The Not-for-Profit
CEO Workbook

The Not-for-Profit CEO Workbook

Practical Steps to Attaining & Retaining the Corner Office

WALTER P. PIDGEON JR.

WILEY

John Wiley & Sons, Inc.

For general information on our other products and services, or technical support,
please contact our Customer Care Department within the United States at 800-762-2974,
outside the United States at 317-572-3993 or fax 317-572-4002.

Wiley also publishes its books in a variety of electronic formats. Some content that
appears in print may not be available in electronic books.

For more information about Wiley products, visit our Web site at http://www.wiley.com.

Library of Congress Cataloging-in-Publication Data:
ISBN-13 978-0-471-76811-1
ISBN-10 0-471-76811-1

10 9 8 7 6 5 4 3 2 1

As is often the case, publications like this and my other books are not the sole result of one person. One of the individuals who has helped make these books a reality through providing editing support has been my son, Walter (BJ) Pidgeon, III.

About the Author

Walter (Bud) Pidgeon, Jr. is a recognized authority on how not-for-profit organizations function. He conducts research on the subject and is credited with the first empirical research published on the benefits that volunteering provides to volunteers. He is a published author and consultant in the areas of government relations, volunteering, fundraising, strategic planning, and membership enhancement. Dr. Pidgeon is responsible for the development of a doctorate degree program in association management through a partnership with the Union Institute & University and the American Society of Association Executives.

His previous books include *The University Benefits of Volunteering: A Practical Workbook for Nonprofit Organizations, Volunteers, and Corporations* (1998), *The Legislative Labyrinth: A Map for Not-for-Profits* (2001), and *The Not-for-Profit CEO: How to Attain & Retain the Corner Office* (2004), published by John Wiley & Sons, Inc.

Dr. Pidgeon has had a distinguished career as a not-for-profit leader. He has held positions that require expertise in government relations, finance, membership development, program enhancement, fund raising, meeting planning, education and administration. Dr. Pidgeon is currently president and chief executive officer of the United States Sportsmen's Alliance, a 501(c)4 organization, and chief executive officer of the United States Sportsmen's Alliance Foundation, a 501(c)3 organization. These organizations represent more than 1.5 million outdoor sports enthusiasts and wildlife management officials at both the federal and state levels. These organizations are headquartered in Columbus, Ohio, and their federal affairs office is located in Washington, DC.

Dr. Pidgeon earned his bachelor's degree in human relations and nonprofit administration at Salem International University, Salem, West Virginia. His major was an American Humanics, Inc., sponsored program in Non-profit Administration.

Dr. Pidgeon earned his doctorate in Philanthropy, Leadership and Voluntary Behavioral Studies at the Union Institute & University in Cincinnati, Ohio.

Dr. Pidgeon is certified by the American Society of Association Executives as a Certified Association Executive (CAE). He is also certified by CFRE International as a Certified Fund Raising Executive (CFRE).

Dr. Pidgeon is an active civic leader and a volunteer in a number of professional, business, and social service organizations.

About ASAE & The Center
for Association Leadership

ASAE & The Center for Association Leadership work together to bring the most comprehensive collection of services and resources to association professionals. The American Society of Association Executives is an individual membership organization made up of nearly 23,000 association executives and industry partners representing nearly 12,000 organizations. Its members manage leading trade associations, individual membership societies, and voluntary organizations across the United States and in 50 countries around the globe. ASAE also represents suppliers of products and services to the association community.

The Center for Association Leadership is the premier provider of learning, future focused, and strategic research and knowledge resources and community that challenge and empower association professionals. The Center offers association professionals an impressive array of essential services and resources that identify the path for success. Together, ASAE & The Center provide resources, education, ideas, and advocacy to enhance the power and performance of the association community.

BRAND STATEMENTS

Our Cause (Why We Exist) — We help associations transform society through the power of collaborative action.

Our Value Proposition (What We Do) — We connect great ideas and great people to inspire leadership and achievement in the association community.

Our Promise (How We Serve Our Stakeholders) — To provide exceptional experiences, a vibrant community, and essential tools that make you and your organization more successful.

Our Guarantee—To provide great experiences and essential tools. If any of our programs, products, or services does not fulfill this promise, we will make the situation right or refund your money.

For More Information

The American Society of Association Executives
1575 I Street, NW
Washington, DC 20005
Phone: 202-371-0940
Toll Free: 888-950-2723
Fax: 202-371-8815
www.asaenet.org

The Center for Association Leadership
Ronald Reagan Building and International Trade Center
1300 Pennsylvania Avenue, NW
Washington, DC 20004
Phone: 202-326-9500
Fax: 202-326-0999
www.centeronline.org

NOTE TO THE READER: All forms and material that were previously on a CD-ROM that accompanied this book have been moved to the following web site: http://booksupport.wiley.com

Contents

The Companion Book

THE NOT-FOR-PROFIT CEO: HOW TO ATTAIN & RETAIN THE CORNER OFFICE

The companion book to this workbook, *The Not-for-Profit CEO: How to Attain & Retain the Corner Office,* was published in 2004 by John Wiley & Sons. It is based on the life's work of the author and an extensive research study of not-for-profit CEOs that the author conducted.

The research methodology for the book included conducting personal interviews with various CEOs as well as undertaking the National Study of Not-for-Profit CEOs which obtained the advice and opinions of over 100 CEOs in 26 states and the District of Columbia. The participating CEOs represented a variety of missions and types of organizations including trade associations, professional societies, social service organizations, and other unique organizations.

The book is designed as a core reference work for students, professionals in the field, and chief executive officers who aspire to attain and retain the CEO position. It is also designed to serve the same individuals as a guide for achieving greater leadership opportunities once they have achieved the rank of CEO.

Chapter 1   The Evolution of the Not-for-Profit CEO Position
Details its origins to current challenges faced by CEOs.

Chapter 2   How Not-for-Profit CEOs Attain Their Positions
Outlines what it takes to make it to the corner office.

Chapter 3   How Not-for-Profit CEOs Retain Their Positions
Provides an overview of what it takes to stay in the corner office.

Chief Executive Officers
Who Participated in the National
Study of Not-for-Profit CEOs

Name	Not-for-Profit Organization
Joseph G. Acker	Synthetic Organic Chemical Manufacturers Association
Jack Advent	Ohio Veterinary Medical Association
John Alfano	Association of Ohio Philanthropic Home, Housing & Services for the Aging
Andrea W. Aughenbaugh, CAE	New Jersey State Nurses Association
William M. Babcock	Wisconsin Society of Architects
Mark Barford, CAE	Appalachian Hardwood Manufacturers, Inc.
Alvin M. Bargas	Associated Builders and Contractors Association Pelican Chapter
Ann-Marie Bartels, AAP	Mid-America Payment Exchange
Andrew R. Behrman	Florida Association of Community Health Centers
Barbara Belmont, CAE	American School Food Service Association
Edwin W. Benson, Jr.	Country Music Association
William G. Bishop, III	Institute of Internal Auditors
John O. Boyd, III	Business Professionals of America, Inc.
Betsy Browne	National Council of Examiners for Engineering and Surveying
Anne L. Bryant, Ed.D., CAE	National School Boards Association
Dr. Thomas J. Burkgren	American Association of Swine Veterinarians
James R. Castle	Ohio Hospital Association

Dr. Elizabeth J. Clark	National Association of Social Workers
Bill Connors	National Business Travel Association, Inc.
Ann R. Cox, CAE	American Association of Occupational Health Nurses, Inc.
Alan B. Davis	National Association for Campus Activities
Arthur T. Dean	Community Anti-Drug Coalitions of America (CADCA)
Alice DeForest, CAE	American Academy of Periodontology
Garis F. Distelhorst	Marble Institute of America
Andrew E. Doehrel	Ohio Chamber of Commerce
Karen Dreyer	Ohio Petroleum Marketers & C-Store Association
Mike Duffin	Precision Machined Products Association
Kay C. Durnett	Arkansas State Employees Association
Dr. Glenda Earwood-Smith	National Alpha Lambda Delta
Barry S. Eisenberg, CAE	American College of Occupational and Environmental Medicine
Douglas S. Evans	Ohio Library Council
Marie M. Fallon	National Association of Local Boards of Health
Dr. Alan E. Farstrup	International Reading Association
David W. Field, CAE	Accent on Management
Katherine Mandusic Finley, CAE, CFRE, CMP	Association for Research on Nonprofit Organizations & Voluntary Action
Brian Fitzgerald	Easter Seal New Jersey
Richard L. Forman	Associated General Contractors of New Jersey
Donald L. Frendberg	Heating, Airconditioning & Refrigeration Distributors International
William F. Fulginiti	New Mexico Municipal League
Bill Gaskin	Precision Metalforming Association
Roger R. Geiger	NFIB-Ohio
William A. Good, CAE	National Roofing Contractors Association
Robert K. Goodwin	Points of Light Foundation
John H. Graham, IV	American Society of Association Executives
Owen Graham	Alaska Forest Association
Albert C. Gray, Ph.D., PE, CAE	National Society of Professional Engineers
Ann Guiberson, PRP, CAE	Pinellas Suncoast Association of Realtors, Inc.
Phillip A. Gutt, CAE	Association Managers, Inc.
Glenn F. Harvey	The American Ceramic Society
Ruth D. Henning	Firelands Association of Realtors, Inc.
Wayne N. Holliday	American Society for Nondestructive Testing
Alberta E. Hultman, CAE	USFN—America's Mortgage Banking Attorneys

Thomas S. Jackson, CAE	Ohio Grocers Association
Allen James, CAE	Responsible Industry for a Sound Environment
Jady Johnson	Reading Recovery Council of North America
Rob Keck	The National Wild Turkey Federation, Inc.
John H. Klesch	Vermont Retail Association
Anne H. LeClair, CAE	San Mateo County Convention and Visitors Bureau
Larry L. Long	County Commissioners Association of Ohio
Mac MacArthur	Alabama State Employees Association
Paulette V. Maehara, CFRE, CAE	Association of Fundraising Professionals
Anna Marie Mason	Society for Computer Applications in Radiology
Kevin McCray, CAE	National Ground Water Association
Dr. Anne W. Miller	Association of School Business Officials International
D. Alex Mills	Texas Alliance of Energy Producers
Brent Mulpren	Ohio State Medical Association
Allen E. Murfin, CAE	Southwest Hardware & Implement Association
Algie Hill Neill	Alabama State Chiropractic Association
James L. Nell	Rental Housing Association of Puget Sound
Joann Ort	Ohio State Health Network
Jerry S. Panz, RCE, CAE	Wilmington Regional Association of Realtors
Phillip L. Parker, CAE, CCE	Dayton Area Chamber of Commerce
Alexander D. Perwich, II	Golden Key International Honour Society
Rodney K. Pierini	California Automotive Wholesalers Association
C. Allen Powell	National Technical Honor Society
Suanne M. Powell	Ohio Fire Chiefs' Association
Alan T. Rains, Jr.	Family Career and Community Leaders of America, Inc.
Michael O. Ranney	Ohio Psychological Association
Alan H. Richardson	American Public Power Association
Beth Risinger	International Executive Housekeepers Association
Carla Roehl, JD, CAE, RCE, CMP	Cleveland Area Board of Realtors
Amy Rohling	Ohio Association of Free Clinics
Roy Rushing	Ohio Gas Association
Anthony Schopp	Savannah Area Convention and Visitors Bureau
Gary J. Schwarzmueller	Association of College and University Housing Officers
John P. Shumate	American Foreign Service Protective Association
Ann M. Spicer	Ohio Academy of Family Physicians
Mary R. Tebeau, CAE	Associated Builders & Contractors, Inc.

Laura L. Tiberi	American College of Emergency Physicians, Ohio Chapter
Albert E. Trexler III, CAE	Pennsylvania Institute of Certified Public Accountants
Ann T. Turner, Ph.D., CAE	American Association for Laboratory Animal Science
Kelly M. Wettengel	American Board of Bariatric Medicine
Jon F. Wills	Ohio Osteopathic Association
Jeannine Windbigler	Office Business Center Association International
Susan F. Wooley	American School Health Association
Katherine Williams Wright, CAE	The Ohio College Association, Inc.
Roy L. Williams	Boy Scouts of America
Sandra L. Yost, MBA	American Academy of Disability Evaluating Physicians

Preface

I began the preface to my third book, *The Not-for-Profit CEO: How to Attain & Retain the Corner Office,* by saying that the chief executive officer (CEO) position of a not-for-profit organization is one of the most exciting positions to hold if you really want to make a difference. This is absolutely true.

I can attest to this fact based both my personal experience as a CEO as well as from the data I have acquired from my research over the years. Being a CEO of a not-for-profit provides a rare opportunity to lead and, at the same time, to truly make a lasting difference.

I have sat in the corner office for 25 years at four different organizations. The missions of each of these organizations were very dissimilar, yet the methods I used to attain and retain these positions were quite similar in nature. The methods I developed were not written or revealed to me directly; rather, they were obtained through personal experiences and the advice I acquired from others who had taken a similar journey in the past.

This journey can be quite a lonely and isolating experience. Often it is filled with those who may wish you well but, at the same time, it may also be filled with those who may not wish you well. In any case, it is rare to find someone who will tell you directly how it is done or someone who has all the answers.

Today, particularly in the not-for-profit field, there is a dire need for true leaders, leaders who believe in the mission of the organizations that they lead and who are willing to take calculated risks to not just fulfill those missions but to exceed them.

To both attract potential leaders and to encourage current not-for-profit professionals to strive for greater leadership opportunities, I felt that a system needed to be created that would set the standard on how to attain and retain a CEO position in a not-for-profit. My book *The Not-for-Profit CEO: How to Attain & Retain the Corner Office* is the culmination of this dream.

In the process of writing the book, I gathered a great deal of data. As I sifted through these data and reflected on my own personal experiences, I began to think about a process where CEO hopefuls could develop a personal document or reference tool that they could use throughout their careers to help them attain and retain the corner office. During this discovery process, it occurred to me that this tool could be used by anyone who wished to develop a career path based on goals and what he or she wanted to receive from the experience.

As the book was going through the editing stages, naturally, some of the data I collected had to be cut out. Due to space considerations and publishing deadlines, the career document concept was shelved.

My editor at John Wiley & Sons, Susan McDermott, suggested that the unused data and the career document concept were too valuable to scrap. She recommended that a workbook that provided the tools to support the findings and recommendations of the book could act as an implementation vehicle for serious-minded students and professionals who aspire to attain and retain the corner office.

Thus, *The Not-for-Profit CEO Workbook: Practical Steps to Attaining & Retaining the Corner Office* became a reality. The workbook is designed to be a simple and direct tool. It refers to the book in many places, and these references assume that the reader has read or at least has the ability to refer to the book to clarify a statement or a necessary action.

The workbook has been divided into four major sections:

Section 1   Academic Preparation

Section 2   Career Experiences and the Leadership Factor

Section 3   The Process of Getting Things Done

Section 4   The Career Strategic Planner

The entire workbook is designed so that the reader may customize the content. I encourage you to adapt the plan to fulfill your personal needs. To assist in the process, blank copies of the forms and the Career Strategic Planner can be found on the CD-ROM attached to the inside back cover of the workbook.

Life is experienced in stages. At birth we depend entirely on our parents to sustain us. Gradually we become more independent, and, through the years, we begin to pursue our ambitions and hopes. By the time we reach high school, we have formed a unique personality that, in some ways, will guide us in our personal and career aspirations. As we continue to mature, both opportunity and chance become factors in how and where life takes us.

Since each of us travels a unique road in life, a workbook such as this must be flexible enough to anticipate all of these unique variables. The workbook examines five fictitious individuals who are in pursuit of the chief executive officer's position at various times in their careers. It examines the opportunities that they have and details ways to take advantage of these opportunities.

These examples are generalities; in reality, the opportunities these characters have may fall at different times in an individual's experience. Therefore, I encourage you to review all of these examples to ensure that you are in the position to take full advantage of every opportunity that may come your way.

The five fictitious characters are:

Student: Theresa Rodriguez
Age: 17
High school junior

Student: Lewis Johnston
Age: 20
College sophomore

Not-for-Profit Professional: Frank Fulton
Age: 36
Vice President Government Relations,
New Jersey Society of Home Growers

For-Profit Executive: Janet McGuire
Age: 43
Vice President of Sales, The Value Group

Not-For-Profit Professional: Ralph Moore
Age: 51
President and CEO, Youth Center, Inc.

It is my hope that this workbook will provide readers who aspire to attain and retain a CEO position with the tools needed to fulfill that dream. If you work wisely, that dream is attainable.

Acknowledgments

A publication of this kind is not created by one person. From the beginning, I relied on a number of people to make this book a reality.

First of all, I would like to thank everyone at John Wiley & Sons, particularly Susan McDermott, Senior Editor, and Kerstin Nasdeo, Senior Production Editor, for the support they provided from believing in the project to helping me to produce this book.

I would also like to thank the leadership of the American Society of Association Executives (ASAE) for their support. Greta Kotler, CAE, Vice President, Professional Development & Credentialing, supported me in conducting the National Study of Not-for-Profit CEOs. John Graham III, President and CEO, believed enough in this project to provide the foreword to the book and helped to make this publication available through ASAE.

I would like to thank Michael Faulkner and Jimelle Rumberg. I had the privilege to serve on both of their doctoral committees, and both of these individuals have provided key information and access to make this publication complete.

I would also like to thank the U.S. Sportsmen's Alliance staff members who supported this effort, including Connie Myers, Executive Secretary; Christy Marler, Fundraising Coordinator; and a special thank-you to Patty Leffler, Marketing Coordinator, for the graphics work.

One of the major reasons that I am able to continue to work on research and publishing projects like this is the love and support that my family provides through encouragement and direct help. A special thank-you to my elder son, Walter (BJ) Pidgeon III, for providing editing support; your expertise really made a difference. To my younger son, Spencer W. Pidgeon, thank you for your support; and to my wife, Susan W. Pidgeon, thank you for your support, constant encouragement, and devotion.

Finally, I would like to thank every not-for-profit CEO who participated in the two formal studies and the hundreds of other CEOs from whom I received advice and encouragement during the two and half years this project took. I hope that you are satisfied with the results.

A Sense of History

In the companion book, *The Not-for-Profit CEO: How to Attain & Retain the Corner Office,* Chapter 1, "The Evolution of the Not-For-Profit CEO," details the origins of the not-for-profit CEO. This is an important chapter to understand for every individual who aspires to become a not-for-profit CEO including students, professionals in the field, for-profit executives who seek a not-for-profit CEO position, and not-for-profit CEOs who wish to attain even greater leadership opportunities. Knowing and understanding the origins of the not-for-profit community as well as grasping how the CEO position is evolving will give CEO candidates a much better chance of attaining and retaining the Corner Office.

The link to present-day not-for-profits can be traced to the beginning of human-kind. Groups or associations fulfill a fundamental function in society that is as natural as life itself. Organizations bring individuals together for a common purpose. Not-for-profits provide a safe haven, including strength in numbers, and they provide a natural outlet for imagination and innovation to flourish.

From the fundamental needs of the first inhabitants on Earth to the multitude of needs of present day society, group activity has been the preferred method for humans to succeed. The key to the success of each group is directly linked to the quality and dynamics that its respective leader possesses.

Group activity has taken many forms as humans became civilized. The introduction of democracy in the United States after the Revolutionary War greatly helped in the acceleration of the development of the not-for-profit sector.

Today, the not-for-profit sector is enormous. According to the Independent Sector's most recent report on the status of the not-for-profit sector, *The New Nonprofit Almanac in Brief,* 1.2 million not-for-profit organizations exist in the United States with the IRS designations of 501(c)3 and 501(c)4. These groups employ 10.6 million workers and have a combined revenue of over $664.8 billion. They employ 7.1 percent of the work force and represent 6.1 percent of the national income.

In addition, the report indicates that 44 percent of the population, or over 89 million adults, volunteer. This is the equivalent of more than 9 million full-time employees at a value of $239 billion. More than 89 percent of households donate to not-for-profits and the average contribution is $1,620.

In addition to these organizations, according to the North American Industrial Classification System, over 100,000, 501(c)6, civic and social organizations, or professional and trade associations exist in America.

The bottom line is that the not-for-profit sector is a major factor in the social and economic success of the United States.

In the beginning not-for-profits were run entirely by volunteers. As the organizations grew, volunteers began to realize that they could not devote the necessary time to the mission and/or that they lacked the expertise to run the organizations. As a result, part-time and, eventually, full-time employees were hired.

As the not-for-profit grew and matured, they began to appoint individuals to oversee the administration of the organization. In many cases, the individual was given the title of 'secretary.' This title was still in use as late as the mid-twentieth century to identify the top professional leader in the not-for-profit. Clearly, the volunteer leaders had absolute power in these organizations during this era.

The top administrator in today's not-for-profit has a number of titles including president, executive vice president, executive director, chief staff officer, and chief executive officer. The title of president and chief executive officer really best reflects the current and future role of the top professional leader of a not-for-profit.

The CEO's role of today is a really a hybrid—it is a careful blend of the not-for-profit traditions of the past combined with many of the characteristics of a for-profit CEO. This blend reflects the increased role that CEOs must play in a not-for-profit. CEOs need to focus on achieving the core mission of the organization while making sure that fiscal integrity is maintained. In addition, the relationship of the CEO with the volunteer leadership has been transformed into a partnership.

The future role of the not-for-profit CEO will continue to change as the wants and needs of the not-for-profit community change. Candidates for these positions will need an extensive education as well as a wealth of experience and skills to meet these future challenges.

At the same time, successful CEOs cannot forget the past. A clear understanding of the origins of the not-for-profit community and a keen awareness of the historical context in which not-for-profits exist will provide a deeper belief in the unique and vital role played by not-for-profits.

Academic Preparation

Destiny is not a matter of chance, it is a matter of choice; it is not a thing to be waited for, it is a thing to be achieved.

—William Jennings Bryan

INTRODUCTION

A growing number of individuals entering the not-for-profit profession are doing so right out of college. A number of these individuals have prepared for their careers by taking some coursework, or they may have even majored in not-for-profit administration. This is a sign that the not-for-profit field is slowly becoming a profession.

As the companion book to this workbook, *The Not-for-Profit CEO: How to Attain & Retain the Corner Office,* notes, individuals who find ways to prepare for leadership positions in the not-for-profit field while still in school will find themselves ahead of the pack.

Although this section is aimed at helping high school and college students to better plan for their careers in the not-for-profit field, it can also provide a quick review of the core personal and academic credentials that are needed to be a successful leader in this field.

HIGH SCHOOL PREPARATION

For some people, the light goes on early in life. From a young age they seem to know the career direction that they wish to take. Several opportunities are available for high school students who have already decided to pursue a career in the not-for-profit community.

Meet Theresa Rodriguez: High School Junior

Theresa Rodriguez is currently a high school junior. As you review Theresa's profile outlined in Exhibit 1.1, you will discover that Theresa has a well-rounded life both in and out of school. Although she may not be the top student in her class, she is maintaining an acceptable grade point average and pursuing other interests.

The subjects that she excels in serve as a good background for not-for-profit work. History provides a rich background on events and human interactions. Economics provides a realistic appraisal of what it takes to maintain a quality of life. English is necessary for communicating ideas and achieving goals.

Theresa's extracurricular activities are diverse and show that she is pushing herself mentally and physically. Her outside interests show that she has a good religious and social base and that the reality of her life requires her to work. Her goals in terms of a college search seem to be sound since she has already determined that she wants to pursue a career in a local community organization.

Like most college-bound high school students, Theresa will have several challenges to overcome. These challenges include scoring well on the SAT, being accepted by

---

EXHIBIT 1.1   PROFILE OF THERESA RODRIGUEZ

- High school junior
- Age 17
- Maintaining a B− average
- Subjects that I excel in:
    - History
    - Economics
    - English
    - Social Studies
- Extracurricular Activities:
    - Debating club
    - Women's track team
- Outside Interests:
    - Church-sponsored teen program
    - Part-time job
- College Search Goal: To select the best school that I can to prepare me for a professional career

the school of her choice, and finding the financial means to pay for college. A number of other sources cover these types of challenges, so there is no need to discuss them here. Suffice to say that a student who is serious about pursuing this coursework will be resourceful enough to have the basic credentials to be admitted and to find the money to underwrite the costs through some combination of grants, loans, and working.

Section Four: The Career Strategic Planner, illustrates how Theresa can use a simple method to plan for the first stages of her career from both an academic perspective and a "hands-on" perspective.

Theresa needs to pursue two major areas:

1. Work in the industry, or "try it before you buy it"
2. Seek colleges/universities that offer degree programs in not-for-profit administration

"Try It Before You Buy It"

I am a major advocate of careers in not-for-profit administration, but it is not a profession for everyone. Throughout the course of my career, I have seen hundreds of good, hardworking people become burned out or who just were not suited for this profession. Anyone who is pursuing this (or any) career should give it a try to see if it is right for them.

In Theresa's case, she is a member of a church-sponsored teen program. This is the perfect chance to get experience by asking if she can play a leadership role as a volunteer. An opportunity like this can provide her with insight on what it takes to run such a program. If this opportunity is too close to her friends to be appropriate or if it is unavailable, Theresa can seek hundreds of other community-based programs that can provide similar experiences. In addition, Theresa should investigate other career/job opportunities to round out her search and her background.

Theresa should also seek and secure mentors and advisors who can help her to make sound decisions on how to begin her academic career. By doing so, she may even discover new and more exciting volunteer or work opportunities. This will only strengthen her pursuit of a career in the not-for-profit community. The companion book to this workbook, *The Not-for-Profit CEO: How to Attain & Retain the Corner Office,* has a number of references on how to attract and get the most out of mentors.

Higher Education Avenues to Pursue

Although Theresa can pursue her degree at many schools, the reality is that financial circumstances often place limitations on what college she will be able to attend. One of the most important search criteria for Theresa will be finding a college with a degree program in not-for-profit administration. A much larger number of institutions now offer such programs (see Exhibit 1.2).

EXHIBIT 1.2   **PARTIAL LIST OF COLLEGES AND UNIVERSITIES THAT OFFER NOT-FOR-PROFIT ADMINISTRATION COURSES OR DEGREE PROGRAMS**

School	Undergraduate	Graduate
Antioch University (AH)*	X	
Arizona State University	X	X
Auburn University at Montgomery (AH)		X
Austin Peay State University	X	
Azusa Pacific University		X
Babson College	X	
Baylor University	X	
Bennett College	X	
Boston University School of Management		X
Boston University School of Social Work		X
Brandeis University		X
Bucknell University	X	
California State University—Los Angeles	X	
California State University—San Bernardino	X	
California State University—Fresno (AH)	X	
California State University—Hayward		X
California State University—Long Beach	X	
Case Western Reserve University		X
Chicago State University	X	
Clayton College and State University (AH)	X	
Clemson University (AH)	X	
Cleveland State University	X	X
College of Mount Saint Joseph (AH)	X	
Columbia University—School of International and Public Relations		X
Coppin State College (AH)	X	
Crichton College (AH)	X	
CUNY—Baruch	X	X
CUNY—Hunter College		X
DePaul University		X
Eastern Connecticut State University (AH)	X	
Eastern Michigan University (AH)	X	
East Tennessee State University	X	
Eastern College		X

EXHIBIT 1.2   PARTIAL LIST OF COLLEGES AND UNIVERSITIES THAT OFFER NOT-FOR-PROFIT ADMINISTRATION COURSES OR DEGREE PROGRAMS *(Continued)*

School	Undergraduate	Graduate
Florida State University		X
Fordham University	X	
Franklin University	X	
George Mason University	X	X
Georgetown University		X
Georgia College and State University (AH)	X	
Georgia State University		X
Golden Gate University		X
Graceland University (AH)	X	
Grand Valley State University (AH)	X	X
Hamline University		X
Harvard University (AH)		X
High Point University (AH)	X	
Indiana State University (AH)	X	
Indiana University—Bloomington (AH)	X	X
Indiana University of Pennsylvania		X
Indiana University—Center on Philanthropy	X	X
Johns Hopkins University		X
Kansas State University (AH)	X	
Kean University (AH)	X	
Kennesaw State University (AH)		X
Kent State University (AH)		X
Lakeland College (AH)	X	
Lesley College		X
Lindenwood University (AH)	X	X
LeMoyne–Owen College (AH)	X	
Long Island University		X
Louisiana State University in Shreveport (AH)	X	
Loyola University Chicago		X
Luther College	X	
Marymount Manhattan College	X	
Maryville College (AH)	X	
Marywood University		X

(continues)

EXHIBIT I.2 **PARTIAL LIST OF COLLEGES AND UNIVERSITIES THAT OFFER NOT-FOR-PROFIT ADMINISTRATION COURSES OR DEGREE PROGRAMS** *(Continued)*

School	Undergraduate	Graduate
Millersville University	X	
Missouri Valley College (AH)	X	
Moorhead State University		X
Murray State University (AH)	X	
New York University—Wagner Graduate School		X
North Carolina Central University	X	
North Dakota State University	X	
North Park University (AH)		X
Northwestern University		X
Oakland College	X	
Oakland University		X
Ohio State University		X
Oklahoma State University (AH)	X	
Oregon State University	X	
Park College		X
Pepperdine University (AH)	X	
Portland State University—Division of Public Administration (AH)		X
Purdue University, Indianapolis (AH)	X	X
Regis University		X
Rhode Island College		X
Robert Morris University (AH)	X	
Roberts Wesleyan College	X	X
Rockhurst University (AH)	X	
Roosevelt University	X	X
Rhode Island College		X
Rutgers University—Camden College	X	
Rutgers University—Newark		X
Saint Mary's University of Minnesota		X
San Diego State University (AH)	X	
San Francisco State University (AH)	X	X
San Jose State University (AH)	X	
Seton Hall University (AH)	X	X
Shaw University (AH)	X	

EXHIBIT 1.2 PARTIAL LIST OF COLLEGES AND UNIVERSITIES THAT OFFER NOT-FOR-PROFIT ADMINISTRATION COURSES OR DEGREE PROGRAMS *(Continued)*

School	Undergraduate	Graduate
Siena College	X	
Slippery Rock University (AH)	X	
South Dakota State University (AH)	X	
Southern Adventist University (AH)	X	
Southern Connecticut State University		X
Southern Illinois University—Edwardsville	X	X
Spertus Institute of Jewish Studies		X
St. Olaf College	X	
St. Louis University		X
St. Louis University—School of Social Work		X
SUNY University at Albany		X
SUNY University at Buffalo (AH)		X
SUNY University at Oneonta (AH)	X	
SUNY University at Oswego	X	
Temple University		X
Union Institute & University	X	X
University of Akron	X	X
University of Alabama at Birmingham		X
University of Baltimore (AH)	X	
University of Arkansas at Little Rock (AH)	X	
University of California at Berkeley	X	X
University of Central Florida (AH)	X	
University of Colorado		X
University of Colorado at Denver		X
University of Connecticut		X
University of the District of Columbia (AH)	X	
University of Dallas		X
University of Florida (AH)	X	
University of Georgia	X	
University of Houston—Victoria	X	
University of Houston (AH)	X	
University of Illinois at Urbana		X
University of Judaism	X	X
University of Maryland		X

(continues)

EXHIBIT I.2   **PARTIAL LIST OF COLLEGES AND UNIVERSITIES THAT OFFER NOT-FOR-PROFIT ADMINISTRATION COURSES OR DEGREE PROGRAMS** *(Continued)*

School	Undergraduate	Graduate
University of Massachusetts		X
University of Memphis (AH)	X	X
University of Michigan School of Social Work		X
University of Minnesota—Humphrey Institute		X
University of Missouri at Kansas City (AH)		X
University of Missouri at St. Louis	X	X
University of Montana (AH)	X	
University of Nebraska (AH)	X	X
University of New Haven (AH)	X	
University of North Carolina—Greensboro	X	X
University of North Carolina—Chapel Hill		X
University of North Carolina—Chapel Hill, Social Work		X
University of North Dakota (AH)	X	
University of Northern Colorado (AH)	X	
University of Northern Iowa (AH)	X	X
University of Northern Texas (AH)	X	
University of Pittsburgh		X
University of San Diego (AH)	X	
University of San Francisco	X	X
University of Southern California	X	X
University of South Carolina (AH)	X	
University of Southern Mississippi (AH)	X	
University of St. Thomas—Center for Nonprofit Management		X
University of St. Thomas—Political Science	X	
University of Tennessee—Chattanooga	X	
University of Texas at San Antonio (AH)	X	
University of Texas at Tyler	X	
University of the District of Columbia	X	
University of the Pacific	X	
University of Vermont	X	
University of Washington MPA Program		X
University of Washington—Tacoma	X	
University of Washington School of Social Work		X
University of West Florida		X

School	Undergraduate	Graduate
Virginia Commonwealth University (AH)	X	X
Walsh University	X	
Wayne State University	X	
Western Kentucky University (AH)	X	
Western Michigan University (AH)		X
William Jewell College (AH)	X	
Wright State University—Liberal Arts (AH)	X	
Widener University		X
Xavier University of Louisiana (AH)	X	
Yeshiva University		X
Youngstown State University (AH)	X	

EXHIBIT 1.2   PARTIAL LIST OF COLLEGES AND UNIVERSITIES THAT OFFER NOT-FOR-PROFIT ADMINISTRATION COURSES OR DEGREE PROGRAMS (Continued)

Source: Roseanne M. Mirabella, *Nonprofit Management Education: Current Offerings in University Based Programs,* Department of Political Science, Seton Hall University, South Orange, NJ, last revision September 10, 2002; and American Humanics, Inc., *Campus Affiliates,* March 11, 2004.
*American Humanics Campus Affiliate

In addition, Theresa has also chosen to investigate schools that are affiliated with American Humanics, Inc. American Humanics provides significant support to many not-for-profit administration degree programs, supporting both the schools themselves and college students by helping them to prepare for their careers and helping them find their first positions in the not-for-profit community.

Theresa was able to find information on American Humanics–sponsored programs by contacting them at:

American Humanics, Inc.
4601 Madison Avenue
Kansas City, MO 64112
800-531-6466
www.humanics.org

COLLEGE CHOICES

Some college students have a general idea of what career they wish to pursue after graduation, but most do not. Many select a general major, such as business administration, and begin to take the general required coursework that often takes two or more years to complete. During the second or third year of college, a light goes on for many students. It occurs to them that in a year or two they will be graduating and that they need to make a decision.

Often this decision is not based on sound judgment. This is one of the most important personal choices that an individual ever makes, so why is the decision seemingly made so casually? It is vitally important to weigh the options and get all the facts. How can you test the waters? Start by doing a little research. Find out:

- Does your current university offer a not-for-profit administration degree program?

- If not, does your institution at least offer a course or two in not-for-profit administration?

- If not, does a nearby university offer a degree program or, at least, a couple of courses?

- If not, does your college or a nearby school offer courses that, while not focused on not-for-profit administration, at least provide a good base to work from?

- If not, are there nearby outside opportunities to support your educational needs?

- If not, should you transfer to a different school altogether?

Meet Lewis Johnston: College Sophomore

Lewis Johnston is a college sophomore and is beginning to investigate careers in not-for-profit administration. As you review Lewis's background in Exhibit 1.3, you will notice that he, like Theresa, has a well-rounded academic and personal background.

In Lewis's case, the logical place to begin his search is at his current university. Lewis can start by visiting his advisor to determine if his school offers a not-for-profit administration degree program and, if so, who would be best to discuss the program with him in detail.

If his university does not offer a degree in this area, maybe it offers a course or two on the subject. Often these courses are not in the catalog, or they may not be accredited. These courses may be offered at night, for example, to attract local community involvement. If they are available, they are a great opportunity to discover if a not-for-profit career is worth pursuing.

If his university does not offer coursework in not-for-profit administration, perhaps a nearby college does. If so, Lewis can take a course or two or even transfer to this college once he decides that he wants to pursue this field.

Even if Lewis cannot find courses that are specific to not-for-profit administration, there are surely courses that have a direct or indirect relationship to not-for-profit

---

EXHIBIT 1.3   PROFILE OF LEWIS JOHNSTON

- College sophomore
- Age 20
- Maintaining a B average
- Subjects that I excel in:
  - Public Speaking
  - American History
  - Spanish
- Extracurricular Activities:
  - Baseball team
  - Community service club
  - ROTC
- Outside Interests:
  - Part-time job
  - Volunteer for a neighborhood PAL program as a baseball coach
- Career Pursuit: To discover a professional career in which I could not only work with people but make a difference as well.

---

coursework. Although having a degree in not-for-profit administration is certainly ideal, particularly in the beginning of a career, the National Study of Not-for-Profit CEOs indicated that the area of discipline of a candidate's academic major really does not make much of a difference in how or why the person is successful as a CEO. In fact, the top five degrees of the CEOs who participated in the study had only an indirect relationship at best to not-for-profit administration. They were:

1. Business/business administration
2. English and/or journalism
3. Health and science fields
4. Education
5. Law

Even if Lewis is able to seek a not-for-profit administration degree as a major, it still may be advisable to seek another discipline as a minor. No one can foresee the future to know what the job market may be like or how his or her career may change. By having other skills and being more familiar with other disciplines, Lewis may have opportunities in both the not-for-profit and for-profit arenas. Focused academic work can provide an edge, but a more "generic" degree may be a logical choice for several reasons, including geography, costs, opportunities, and overall career goals.

Even if Lewis is unable to attend a school offering a not-for-profit administration degree program or courses in not-for-profit management, all is not lost. He still can focus on gaining a good academic background, and he still can pursue volunteer opportunities in the field.

Lewis can focus on more traditional degrees and gain not-for-profit skills from other avenues. Many degree programs can provide an excellent base in the not-for-profit world, including:

- Business administration
- Political science
- Liberal arts
- Public administration
- Sociology

Additional coursework taken as a second major, a minor, or even as electives can provide an even stronger base in the not-for-profit world. Areas that are valuable include:

- History
- Public speaking
- Business management
- Accounting
- Communications
- Computer information systems
- English
- Finance
- Economics
- Foreign languages
- Philosophy
- Business law
- Psychology
- Marketing

Although the National Survey of Not-for-Profit CEOs concluded that the academic backgrounds of current CEOs have not traditionally been a major factor in their overall success, the percentage of professionals who are earning a degree specifically in not-for-profit administration is increasing dramatically. Your choice of a major will not determine how well you will do in the not-for-profit community; however, a not-for-profit administration degree can provide a measurable advantage as you enter the profession.

If Lewis chooses a more traditional degree rather than one in not-for-profit administration, he would be best served to pursue as many outside opportunities as possible to gain experience in the not-for-profit field. His profile indicates that he is involved with a community service club at college and that he is a volunteer baseball coach for the PAL program. These are two obvious activities he can pursue for additional experience. Lewis may also want to seek a part-time job in a not-for-profit organization to gain direct insight on how these groups function.

Lewis should also become acquainted with the various types of tax-exempt organizations as defined by the U.S. Internal Revenue Code. Although most organizations that employ a full-time staff fall under three classifications—(501(c)3, 501(c)4, and 501(c)6)—there are actually 39 different classifications. Exhibit 1.4 contains a detailed list. All of these organizations have potential career opportunities, and Lewis's goals and desires may be best suited for a particular type.

EXHIBIT 1.4   TYPES OF TAX-EXEMPT ORGANIZATIONS AS DEFINED BY THE U.S. INTERNAL REVENUE CODE

IRS Section	Classification
501(c)(1)	Government instrumentality
501(c)(2)	Title-holding corporation
501(c)(3)	Educational organization
	Literary organization
	Organization to prevent cruelty to animals
	Organization to prevent cruelty to children
	Organization for public safety testing
	Religious organization
	Scientific organization
501(c)(4)	Civic league
	Local association of employees
	Social welfare organization
501(c)(5)	Agriculture organization
	Horticulture organization
	Labor organization
501(c)(6)	Board of trade
	Business league
	Chambers of Commerce
	Real estate board
501(c)(7)	Pleasure, recreational or social club
501(c)(8)	Fraternal beneficiary society, order, or association
501(c)(9)	Voluntary employee beneficiary associations (nongovernment)

(continues)

EXHIBIT I.4   **TYPES OF TAX-EXEMPT ORGANIZATIONS AS DEFINED BY THE U.S. INTERNAL REVENUE CODE** *(Continued)*

IRS Section	Classification
	Voluntary employee beneficiary associations (government employees)
501(c)(10)	Domestic fraternal societies and associations
501(c)(11)	Teachers' retirement fund associations
501(c)(12)	Benevolent life insurance association
	Mutual ditch or irrigation company
	Mutual or cooperative telephone company
	Organization like those on three preceding lines
501(c)(13)	Burial association
	Cemetery company
501(c)(14)	Credit union
	Other mutual corporation or association
501(c)(15)	Mutual insurance company or association other than life or marine
501(c)(16)	Corporation financing crop operation
501(c)(17)	Supplemental unemployment compensation trust or plan
501(c)(18)	Employee-funded pension plan created before June 25, 1959
501(c)(19)	Posts or organizations of war veterans
501(c)(20)	Legal service (obsolete)
501(c)(21)	Black lung
501(c)(22)	Multiemployer pensions plan
501(c)(23)	Veterans organizations founded prior to 1880
501(c)(24)	Trust described in section 4049 of ERISA
501(c)(25)	A holding company for pensions
501(c)(26)	State-sponsored high-risk health insurance organization
501(c)(27)	State-sponsored workers' compensation reinsurance organization
501(d)	Apostolic and religious organization
501(e)	Cooperative hospital service organization
501(f)	Cooperative service organization of operating education organizations
501(k)	Child care under 501(k)
501(n)	Charitable risk pool
521	Farmers' cooperative
529	Qualified state-sponsored tuition
527	Political organizations
4947(a)(2)	Nonexempt charitable trust 4947(a)(2) (split interest)
4947(a)(1)	Nonexempt charitable trust (public charity)
4947(a)(1)	Nonexempt charitable trust (trust treated as private foundation)
1381(a)(2)	Taxable farmers' cooperative

Source: Internal Revenue Service Exhibit 25.7.2-2, (12-01-2002), Table of EO Subsection and Classification Codes.

SUMMARY

The National Study of Not-for-Profit CEOs revealed a number of significant findings concerning academic preparation for careers in not-for-profit administration. The detailed results can be found in the companion book, *The Not-for-Profit CEO: How to Attain & Retain the Corner Office*. While 99 percent of the CEOs who participated in the study had earned college degrees, it is significant to note that 66 percent also earned graduate degrees. Of the 66 percent with graduate degrees, nearly 16 percent had earned a doctorate degree.

This is strong evidence that academic experience and credentialing are key factors in attaining a CEO position in a not-for-profit. At the same time, the study also revealed a broad range of degree disciplines among the participating CEOs. It is important to have a solid academic background, but the field of study is less important in attaining or retaining the CEO position.

The exciting trend in the area of academic preparation is the expansion of degree programs in not-for-profit administration. This is yet one more indication that careers in the not-for-profit sector are gaining a professional status. This is good news. Not-for-profit CEOs probably will continue to have a relatively wide range of academic backgrounds; however, this may be very healthy for our community as they will continue to represent organizations with an equally wide range of missions.

Career Experiences and the Leadership Factor

There is no more noble occupation in the world than to assist another human being, to help someone succeed.

—Alan Loy McGinnis

INTRODUCTION

According to the CEOs who participated in the National Study of Not-for-Profit CEOs, there are three key factors that will affect your bid for the corner office. They are:

1. Integrity/trust

2. Leadership traits

3. Past experience

These three factors far outweigh any other qualities that volunteer boards seek in their CEOs. The details on how aspiring CEOs can gain or nurture these necessary qualities can be found in the companion book, *The Not-for-Profit CEO: How to Attain & Retain the Corner Office.*

It is interesting to note that the first two factors are personal qualities and therefore are within anyone's control. Possessing and refining leadership traits, being a person of integrity, and establishing trust can begin at any age. The last factor, however, is a product of time. Experience takes time and work, and it is earned over the course of a career.

Integrity/trust is the number-one quality that not-for-profit boards of directors seek in their CEOs. These traits come, in part, from within a person, but they are also picked up from loved ones during the formative years. It is these nurturers who train us on these basic principles and qualities of life.

Integrity and trust are immeasurable and unquantifiable, but they are some of the most valuable qualities to possess. Not-for-profit boards seek these traits above all. They seek someone who they can trust in the CEO position. They seek someone who will tell them what is happening—in both good and bad times. They seek someone to recommend solutions to problems as an unbiased party. They seek someone who can lead the organization in reacting to the ever-changing playing field.

People will argue forever about whether someone is born with leadership traits or whether they are acquired skills. The truth is that leadership traits are a blend of both. Not everyone is a born leader; however, most would-be leaders are lost due to a lack of skill enhancement and opportunity.

Anyone with an eye on the corner office should pursue as many leadership opportunities as possible. This includes opportunities in both career and personal settings. Opportunities are present in your current working environment, through other organizations, within your community, or in everyday life experiences. When you actively begin to hone your leadership traits, you will be amazed at how many more opportunities suddenly come your way.

Experience can be acquired only by being in the game. This sounds rather simple but, in reality, there are very few who actually play the game. If you want to be one of the players, you need to realize that CEOs who attain and retain the corner office must have the necessary experience to understand the everyday ins-and-outs of running a successful organization, as well as the long-range perspective needed to maintain and predict success.

All aspiring CEOs need to take the time to examine themselves to determine if they are truly suited to become a CEO of a not-for-profit organization. This is the time to be completely honest with yourself. The corner office is not for everyone. Exhibit 2.1 will help you to determine if you are made of the right stuff.

PROFESSIONALS IN THE FIELD

Professional CEOs come from a variety of disciplines. Most had no idea that they would be working for a not-for-profit when they were in college. This is due to a number of factors. Many of these professionals fulfill roles that are also found in for-profits, including areas such as finance, communications, and marketing. Even those who perform duties in areas such as administration, fundraising, meeting planning, membership services, or volunteer management may have adapted these skills from their time in for-profits or simply from learning how to do a job to pay the bills.

With all of that said, I have found that individuals who tend to stay in the not-for-profit community have an innate, or at least acquired, dedication to both the

EXHIBIT 2.1   ARE YOU CEO MATERIAL?

Find out if you are CEO material by asking yourself the following questions.

1. What is the highest academic degree you wish to earn?
   - ❏ AA
   - ❏ BA/BS
   - ❏ Master's
   - ❏ Doctorate
   - ❏ Other; please explain: _____

2. How many hours a week do you prefer to work?
   - ❏ 30 hours
   - ❏ 40 hours
   - ❏ 50 hours
   - ❏ Other; please explain: _____

3. How do you or would you describe your main career objective?
   Select one answer:
   - ❏ To provide income for my needs
   - ❏ To do something that I enjoy
   - ❏ A way to make a difference
   - ❏ Other; please explain: _____

4. Do you understand the fundamental principles of accounting and finance?
   _____ (Yes or no).

5. Do you volunteer? _____ (Yes or no); if yes, how often?
   - ❏ Once a year
   - ❏ Once a month
   - ❏ Once a week
   - ❏ Other; please explain: _____

   Have you ever managed volunteers? _____ (Yes or no); if yes, how often:

   _____

6. Have you ever been in a leadership position? _____ (Yes or no). How did you enjoy the experience? Please rank (1 to 5, 1 being the highest level): _____

7. Do you have an understanding of the representative form of government?
   _____ (Yes or no).

(continues)

EXHIBIT 2.1   ARE YOU CEO MATERIAL? *(Continued)*

Have you ever participated in any election or cause related campaign at the local, state, or federal level: _____ (Yes or no).

If so, did you enjoy the experience? _____ (Yes or no).

8. Do you enjoy dealing with a diverse array of people? _____ (Yes or no).

9. Have you ever raised funds for a charity? _____ (Yes or no).

If so, did you enjoy doing it? _____ (Yes or no).

10. How many times have you spoken before a group? _____

If you have spoken before a group, how did you feel about these experiences?

❏ I liked it.

❏ I may want to do it again.

❏ I loved it; can't wait to do it again.

Are You CEO Material? Answers

1. Although a number of CEOs hold undergraduate degrees, the demand for higher educational degrees will continue to build. Of the CEOs who participated in the National Study of Not-for-Profit CEOs, 66 percent had earned advanced degrees.

2. Other: 50 hours a week for CEOs is rare; it is more like 60+ hours.

3. A way to make a difference: The role of a CEO is very demanding. If you are in it just to pick up a paycheck, you are in the wrong business.

4. Yes: CEOs are required to know how to manage the fiscal part of the operation.

5. Yes: Successful CEOs volunteer for all kinds of things. It keeps them out in the real world, and they bring new and better ideas back to their associations. Managing volunteers is one of the major roles of CEOs. They try to multiply what they do a thousandfold.

6. Yes: Successful CEOs are leaders, not managers. Those who enjoy leading make very good CEOs.

7. Yes: CEOs need to both understand and enjoy working in the government affairs arena.

8. Yes: CEOs deal with all kinds of people; they need to love the process.

9. Yes: Raising revenue from fundraising or securing memberships is part of the CEOs' game plan. The more they raise, the more they can accomplish. Knowing how it's done and, more importantly, wanting to be a core player in the process is key to the success of a CEO of a not-for-profit organization.

10. Many times—I loved it; can't wait to do it again. Speaking on behalf of the not-for-profit that you represent is a vital part of the CEO's role.

organization that they serve and to the overall not-for-profit field. As with most jobs, each of these employees seems to fit into one category:

- Some are satisfied to work 40 hours a week doing a routine job.
- Others enjoy their narrow area of specialization and give everything to that discipline.
- Others want to move up the ladder but do not wish to seek the CEO position.
- A select few actively seek the corner office.

Every employee plays a vital and important role in maintaining the current health and success of a not-for-profit organization. The CEO must look to the horizon to gauge the future while, at the same time, motivate each of these types of employees to do their best.

All employees, no matter what role they play, must be nurtured. Employees who only wish to hold routine jobs need to be motivated to keep on the cutting edge and be reminded of the role they fulfill. Employees who specialize in a particular area, such as finance or government relations, must be reminded of how their job fits in with the overall mission of the organization. Employees who move into management roles need to be nurtured into being the key players in moving the organization forward. Employees who seek the corner office can be very valuable to the current CEO so long as there is a trust factor.

Aspiring CEOs need to play the game the right way—the earlier you start in your career, the better your chances. This does not mean trying to unseat your current CEO or finding ways to do the same at another organization. It is the last thing you would want as a CEO, and it is simply unethical. An ethical professional seeking to become a CEO of a not-for-profit should seek help from everyone, including the current CEO. If you approach this situation correctly and if the current CEO is both confident and generous, it will be a wonderful experience and you will have a mentor for life.

Meet Frank Fulton: Professional in the Field

The third example is Frank Fulton. Frank is the vice president of government relations for the New Jersey Society of Home Growers. As Exhibit 2.2 reveals, Frank has had a successful not-for-profit career as a professional. He also has other interests that involve his family, community, and personal avocations. This makes him a well-rounded person, and it may provide clues about what types of future CEO positions he may be best suited for. Section 4, The Career Strategic Planner, reveals that the best career position match is often rooted in the personal interests of the candidate.

EXHIBIT 2.2   PROFILE OF FRANK FULTON

- Age: 36
- Married with three children
- Earned BA degree in Recreational Management
- Career History: Tenure as a not-for-profit professional—12 years
    - Assistant Director of Communications—Iowa Restaurant Association
    - Director of Field Services—Virginia Association of the Blind
    - Vice President of Government Relations—New Jersey Society of Home Growers
- Professional Organizations:
    - American Society of Association Executives (ASAE)
    - Past member of two ASAE allied groups—current officer of NJSAE
- Career Training:
    - Career education in association management
    - Public speaking
- Certifications:
    - Certified Association Executive (CAE)
    - Certified Meeting Planner (CMP)
- Outside Interests:
    - Football coach for middle son's team
    - Plays drums part time for a rock band
    - Volunteer officer in a community social service organization

Before Frank conducts a formal search for a possible CEO position, he should complete the Not-for-Profit CEO Position Self-Evaluation Form for Professionals in the Field. This form should be based on his Career Strategic Planner. The form provides an opportunity for Frank to evaluate six items before beginning the search:

1. The qualities that he can bring to the table
2. Any areas that he may wish to enhance before beginning the search
3. The areas in which he has limited knowledge
4. The types of work that he does not wish to perform
5. The types of CEO positions he would like to seek
6. The ideal CEO position he wishes to pursue

Frank's completed self-evaluation form is shown in Exhibit 2.3. A blank form for your use can be found on the CD-ROM that accompanies this workbook.

EXHIBIT 2.3   THE NOT-FOR-PROFIT CEO POSITION SELF-EVALUATION FORM FOR PROFESSIONALS IN THE FIELD

Name: _Frank Fulton_   Date completed: _M/D/Y_

The following is a brief overview of my current self-evaluation to determine if I wish to pursue a CEO position in a not-for-profit.

1. Qualities I bring to the table:
   a. _BA degree in Recreational Management_
   b. _Seasoned not-for-profit professional_
   c. _Work experience with three organizations_
   d. _Certified Association Executive_
   e. _Certified Meeting Planner_
   f. _Keep on the cutting edge through training_
   g. _An officer of NJSAE_
   h. _Volunteer for various community organizations_

2. Areas I need to enhance before I begin my search for a CEO position:
   a. _I may want to complete a master's degree program over the next 18 months. Should I wait to begin my search until then?_

3. My weak areas or fields in which I have limited knowledge:
   a. _Accounting and fiscal management_

4. Types of work I do not wish to perform:
   a. _I do not want to be out of town a great deal due to family obligations._
   b. _I do not want to be office bound, I like the action outside the office._

5. Types of CEO positions I would like to seek:
   a. _I would like to discover a CEO position that relates to my recreational training and part-time interests._
   b. _If that is not possible, perhaps I could find a CEO position that represents musical interests._

6. Profile of the ideal CEO position I wish to seek:
   a. _I seek a CEO position in an association in my general locale._
   b. _It must be large enough to have support staff who do most office functions._
   c. _I want to be able to have enough time to pursue outside interests, including coaching my son's football team and to be home most nights._
   d. _The organization that I seek must have a mission that I can support._
   e. _I am looking for an organization that understands the proper roles that members, volunteers, staff, and the CEO play to generate a real team effort._

Based on my evaluation, I estimate that my search can begin: _M/D/Y_

Signature: _Frank Fulton_

Question 1: Determining the Qualities That He Can Bring to the Table
Frank has a number of attributes that will qualify him to become a CEO. These include a BA degree as well as a wealth of past experience in the not-for-profit field in the areas of communications, staff management, and government relations. Frank's varied background will make him a very desirable CEO candidate to a number of search committees.

Frank is also certified in the two critical areas: association management and meeting planning. He has kept up with his career training, which is an important asset for volunteer leaders who seek CEOs who are on the cutting edge. He has also been recognized by his peers for his work as exemplified by his role as an officer in the New Jersey Society of Association Executives (NJSAE) and his active role as a volunteer in community organizations.

Question 2: Discovering Any Areas That He May Wish to Enhance Before Beginning the Search   Frank feels that he might want to complete his master's degree before he begins his search. Although this is a noble idea, it is not wise. A lot of things can happen in the 18 to 24 months it takes to get a master's degree, and it is not a given that Frank will be able to complete it. More important, in the meantime good opportunities are sure to slip by.

If Frank had already been working toward a master's degree, it would be best to make sure to alert prospective search committees to this achievement while still continuing the search for the perfect position. As he has not started his degree work, his best bet is to tell search committees that his goal to complete his degree in, say, the next three years. This will give him ample time to live up to his promise; in the meantime, he has taken advantage of current opportunities. Perhaps his future association may even help underwrite the costs of the degree.

Question 3: Assessing the Areas in Which He Has Limited Knowledge
Frank has a limited knowledge of accounting and fiscal management procedures. This is a major weakness and one that he needs to address. It is crucial for Frank to gain this critical knowledge. His best approach is to take a few courses in accounting and fiscal management and then to ask his current CEO to help him use his new skills in a practical application within his current association. If that is not possible, other local not-for-profits may have a way that Frank can gain practical experience in these areas through volunteering.

Question 4: Enumerating the Types of Work That He Does Not Wish to Perform   Frank is willing to perform whatever tasks are necessary to fulfill the role of any potential CEO position that would be available. However, he would like the position to be as close to home as possible. Although this may limit his opportunities, it will also limit the extent of his search. For example, by limiting his search area, he can scout potential organizations more directly.

Frank also wants a CEO position that will allow him to get out of the office as much as possible. Large organizations with a well-designed governance structure would welcome such an individual since the real work of the CEO is outside the office anyway.

Question 5: Discovering the Types of CEO Positions He Would Like to Seek   Frank is thinking about leading an association in a field that relates to his educational background or interests. Although this is an ideal goal, sometimes it is not realistic. Still, it is a goal worth shooting for. If you are lucky enough to find an organization with a mission that is near and dear to you, it will be a calling, and not work at all.

In Frank's case, his limited search territory may mean having to reassess this goal. However, there may be a regional or state organization that could fulfill his needs and still achieve most of his goals.

Question 6: Profiling the Ideal CEO Position He Wishes to Pursue   Frank expressed a number of personal desires and qualities that he feels should be part of his next CEO position. Although it will be impossible to meet all of his personal needs and to find an organization that possesses all of the qualities he seeks, it is important to compare job opportunities to a standard that you hold. Most CEOs end up compromising with a position that is a bit less than the ideal, but often they find ways to move the group and the CEO role toward their ideal. This is, after all, the role of a successful CEO.

Frank Fulton's professional self-evaluation provided an opportunity for him to reflect on his ideals and the perfect position while, at the same time, allowing him to base his future search on reality. Even though not all of his personal and professional hopes will be fulfilled, the process has helped him to set a standard in which he can conduct his search while revealing the areas that he needs to work on and where he needs to compromise.

For example, Frank concluded that he will postpone his formal search for several months until he has had the time to take a few courses in accounting and fiscal management. This will give him time to work with his current CEO to find ways to apply that knowledge in a practical setting. In the meantime, he can research possible not-for-profits to cultivate.

ENTERING THE NOT-FOR-PROFIT SECTOR FROM THE FOR-PROFIT SECTOR

Most employees in the not-for-profit sector began their career in a for-profit entity. This is important to note because it is easy to forget that the not-for-profit model is, in many ways, copied from the for-profit operation structure. Individuals from the for-profit sector can readily enter the not-for-profit environment and be quite successful. However, these individuals need to be very aware of the fact that the two sectors differ in many ways. To be successful, the for-profit incumbent must know these important differences.

The companion book to this workbook, *The Not-for-Profit CEO: How to Attain & Retain the Corner Office,* details a plan for making a successful transition from a for-profit to a not-for-profit environment. To retain a not-for-profit CEO position, for example, the leader must know which experiences are adaptable from the business world and which ones are not. One of the best ways of determining this is by seeking the advice of the right mentors who can help make the transition smoother.

Meet Janet McGuire: A For-Profit Executive

Janet McGuire is the vice president a for-profit entity named the Value Group. This business is located in a major city. Janet's profile can be found in Exhibit 2.4, which shows that she has had a successful career in sales in two for-profit businesses.

There are a number of reasons why a seasoned for-profit executive will choose to seek a CEO position in a not-for-profit. For example, in recent years the for-profit job market has downsized. At the same time, well-paid positions have emerged in the not-for-profit sector. As a result, more for-profit executives are being drawn to seek opportunities in the not-for-profit sector.

In a number of cases, for-profit executives may be sought out for particular not-for-profit CEO positions. For example, trade associations often tap key players from the industry who can represent and lead them.

Janet McGuire has been approached by the local affiliate of the Leukemia Society to consider becoming its next CEO. The current CEO, Jim Bacon, is retiring, and the society seeks someone whom it can trust, someone who has business sense, and someone who understands the organization's needs from a personal standpoint. The current CEO was with the Leukemia Society for 27 years and was their first executive. Jim was drawn to the position due to his son's illness.

Jim has been impressed with Janet's zeal on the board, her work with other volunteers, her ability to raise funds, and her business management skills. Jim and the board chair approached Janet to see if she had an interest.

The offer took Janet by surprise, and she asked the search committee to give her two weeks to think about it. Initially she dismissed the idea outright. The more Janet thought about it, however, the more appeal the idea had.

EXHIBIT 2.4 PROFILE OF JANET MCGUIRE

- Age 43
- Divorced—two children
- Earned MBA
- Career History: Tenure as a for-profit professional—18 years
  - Sales associate—JB Wilson & Company
  - Assistant Branch Manager—Henry Forge, Inc.
  - Branch Manager—Henry Forge, Inc.
  - Director of Regional Sales—The Value Group
  - Vice President of Sales—The Value Group
- Professional Organizations:
  - American Management Association
  - Chamber of Commerce
  - National Association of Wholesaler-Distributors
- Career Training:
  - Various courses in sales and management
- Certifications:
  - None
- Outside Interests:
  - School activities of children
  - Various volunteer positions
  - On the board of the local affiliate of the Leukemia Society due to daughter's disease

Many questions occurred to her as she began to ponder the offer. She decided to analyze the opportunity like any important business decision she had made in the past. Exhibit 2.5 provides the results of her research. A blank self-evaluation form can be found on the CD-ROM that accompanies this text.

To analyze this opportunity, Janet asked herself six very focused questions to determine if she wanted to become the CEO for the local Leukemia Society.

1. Would becoming a not-for-profit CEO be the right move for me?
2. What skills would I bring to the table from my for-profit experience that would set me apart?
3. What skills will I need to leave behind if I accept the not-for-profit CEO position?

4. What new skills would I need to learn to be successful?

5. What are the best methods to market myself for a not-for-profit CEO position?

6. How do I make an objective decision about whether to accept a not-for-profit CEO position?

EXHIBIT 2.5   THE NOT-FOR-PROFIT CEO POSITION SELF-EVALUATOR FOR FOR-PROFIT EXECUTIVES

Name: *Janet McGuire*   Date completed: *M/D/Y*

1. Would becoming a not-for-profit CEO be the right career move for me?
   a. *I do believe in the cause and mission of the Leukemia Society.*
   b. *I would be able to be home more for my children.*
   c. *I always wanted to run my own shop.*
   d. *The compensation level is a consideration; I need to compare it to for-profit companies.*
   e. *Is this a position that I want to do for the next few years, and if I wanted to seek another position someday, would this position help or hinder my career?*

2. What skills would I bring to the table from my for-profit experience that would set me apart?
   a. *My sales experience would help a great deal to increase the organization's visibility and possible bottom line.*
   b. *My management skills could help the society run smoother.*
   c. *My business contacts could attract more volunteers.*
   d. *My ability to network will be an asset.*

3. What skills will I need to leave behind if I accept the not-for-profit CEO position?
   a. *The dog-eat-dog environment in sales would need to be toned down.*
   b. *The method of dealing with those who get things done — employees in for-profit versus volunteers in not-for-profits — would be quite different.*

4. What new skills would I need to learn to be successful?
   a. *Increase my skills of working with diverse people*
   b. *To better understand the workings of the not-for-profit sector*
   c. *To find out the lay of the land both locally and nationally of the Leukemia Society, including how it interacts both within its ranks and to external audiences*

5. What are the best methods to market myself for a not-for-profit CEO position?
   While I have been sought out for the position, I am not sure that I am the only candidate. What will I need to do to set myself apart from the others?

6. How do I make an objective decision about whether to accept a not-for-profit CEO position?
   If the position is presented to me, what criteria will I use to make a wise decision to accept it or not?

Question 1: Would Becoming a Not-for-Profit CEO Be the Right Move for Me?   As Janet began to think about the offer, one of her most important revelations was that she really believed in the cause and mission of the Leukemia Society. This is a very important aspect for considering any position. In my career, I have turned down good positions for organizations that I could never represent. I have also eagerly accepted less than ideal positions for organizations whose cause I believed in.

Janet also saw the personal benefits of being near home. She may find that she is working longer hours, including many nights and weekends; if so, the shorter commute will definitely help.

The thrill of running her own shop was certainly a positive to Janet. Janet felt that her for-profit background would be an asset here. At the same time, she also knew that running such a small organization would be an enormous challenge; she also knew that it that would demand constant attention.

The question of compensation is always a major factor. The Leukemia Society may not be able to match Janet's current level of compensation, but it may be able to provide other benefits or incentives, such as time off or a flexible schedule.

Janet very wisely has decided not to accept the position unless there is a promise that she will be there for a given period of time.

Janet also wants to determine if the position will set the stage for future opportunities. The answer, of course, lies in the plan that she will need to create and execute to cultivate and open doors to new opportunities. Janet's Career Strategic Planner, found in Section Four, demonstrates practical ways of accomplishing her goals.

Question 2: What Skills Would I Bring to the Table from My For-Profit Experience That Would Set Me Apart?   Janet has several skills that she feels will appeal to the search committee. At the top of the list is her sales experience. This could potentially help the society to significantly increase its visibility and increase its fundraising capacity. This is a major need for the Leukemia Society.

Janet's management skills, in particular her knowledge of technologies, would help a great deal in moving the society forward.

Janet also feels that her business contacts would be a great asset in attracting funding and, more important, potential volunteers. She feels that her ability to identify, seek, and add key people to her network is a fundamental skill that would significantly increase the visibility and power of the society.

Question 3: What Skills Will I Need to Leave Behind if I Accept the Not-for-Profit CEO Position?   Janet has given this question a great deal of thought. Few for-profit crossover candidates ask themselves this question. Janet knows that one of the key elements of leading a not-for-profit is finesse. She understands that the dog-eat-dog mind-set of her for-profit sales job may be acceptable in her current position but would not work well in the not-for-profit community.

Competition for volunteers and staff is stronger than ever; however, the manner in which not-for-profits attract good people differs a great deal from how Janet closed deals in the for-profit arena. This is also true of the manner of dealing with the "movers and shakers," the volunteers and employees in not-for-profits. A not-for-profit CEO's success depends on recognizing and knowing these differences.

Question 4: What New Skills Would I Need to Learn to Be Successful?   Janet has wisely perceived that her number-one challenge will be the art and skill of working with people. Although she has worked with a number of people in her sales career, working with the diverse array of people that will make up her new constituency will be more of a challenge.

Janet also realizes that she will need to have a better understanding of the inner workings of the not-for-profit sector. Even though she has been a volunteer for some time, she really does not fully understand how things get done.

Janet also will need to have a better understanding of the Leukemia Society's culture, both at the local and at the national level. Her future may lie in greater professional leadership opportunities with the society, and she knows that it is never too early to begin the cultivation process.

Question 5: What Are the Best Methods to Market Myself for a Not-for-Profit CEO Position?   Janet correctly realizes that, even though she was approached to be a candidate for the CEO position, she may not be the only candidate. Even if she is, she will still need to sell the entire board on her candidacy. With that in mind, Janet set out to find out as much information as possible about the Leukemia Society, both on a local and a national level. She also gathered information on not-for-profits in general.

The companion book to this workbook provides an overview of what is needed to attain a not-for-profit position. It contains several references on the interview process, as well.

Question 6: How Do I Make an Objective Decision About Whether to Accept a Not-for-Profit CEO Position?   Janet developed the criteria she will use to decide whether to accept the CEO position at the Leukemia Society. She feels that it will come down to six factors:

1. Does she believe in the cause and mission of the society enough to lead the organization to the next level?
2. Is she willing to put enough time and energy into the position to be successful?
3. Is she willing to learn the fine differences between a not-for-profit and a for-profit?
4. Is it the right career move?
5. Is she willing to take a pay cut?
6. Is she ready to make a difference?

Janet has an important decision to make. This decision will affect not only her life and career but the lives of everyone involved with the local Leukemia Society. If Janet accepts the position, her success will be linked with how well she leads the society to the next level of service.

NOT-FOR-PROFIT CEOs WHO SEEK A HIGHER LEADERSHIP CALLING

Many of my fellow CEOs have heard the call to higher service. Who will move where and what position will open up next are questions that are asked constantly within our ranks. Over the years, I was caught up with this nonsense like everyone else. As I acquired more gray hair and then as I began to shed that gray hair all together, it dawned on me that this was not a game that CEOs should play.

Being a leader is a privilege. The opportunity to make a difference should be savored rather than squandered for a new position to achieve higher visibility or a few more dollars. The opportunity to serve is more important than engaging in the self-service of hopping from one position to another.

With that said, I have served as the CEO of four not-for-profits, and each experience prepared me for the next. Other CEOs have stayed with one organization for their entire career, building a massive structure stone by stone. There is no real answer to which way is right or wrong. The key to making the decision to seek a higher leadership opportunity must be motivated by the need to serve others from both a personal and professional standpoint.

No one is perfect for every opportunity that comes along, however. Individuals have different skills and personalities. What may serve you well in one organization may have the opposite effect in another.

My current position as CEO of the U.S. Sportsmen's Alliance, for example, is very well suited for me. The skills I brought to the table were skills that were needed. The culture of the organization has always encouraged a team approach between the volunteers and the staff, and this, too, was an ideal fit for my personality and background. When my time to serve is completed, however, will my organization be best served by hiring a CEO with a personality and background similar to mine? Probably not.

The process of matching the best prospective CEO to each not-for-profit is still a game of chance—no matter how well each side prepares. It is important, therefore, that successful CEOs avoid making the common mistake of leaving a position of worth for a CEO role that is not well suited for their talents and wisdom.

At the same time, many good CEOs do need to leave their not-for-profit after a certain period of time, both for the overall health of the organization and for their own personal growth. Deciding when is the right time to leave can be very difficult, particularly if you are comfortable with your current surroundings.

Meet Ralph Moore: A Successful Not-for-Profit CEO

Ralph Moore is currently the CEO of Youth Center, Inc., a regional youth program that has received national praise for its work with inner-city young people. Ralph's profile, shown in Exhibit 2.6, clearly shows that he is a seasoned professional.

Ralph earned his doctorate degree at the age of 40, and he has put this experience to good use by measuring, from a historical perspective, the needs of those he serves. He has also analyzed his work from a more long-term strategic approach. His career spans more than 24 years and includes experience working in youth-related organizations at the grassroots level, directing fundraising functions, overseeing government relations activities, and serving as the CEO of a not-for-profit organization.

EXHIBIT 2.6   PROFILE OF RALPH MOORE

- Age 51
- Single
- Earned Ph.D. in History
- Career History: Tenure as a not-for-profit professional—24 years
  - Assistant District Executive, Boys & Girl Clubs of America
  - District Executive, Boys Clubs of America
  - Fundraising Director, Community Services, Inc.
  - Vice President, Government Relations, Community Services, Inc.
  - President, Youth Center, Inc.
- Professional Organizations:
  - Association of Fund Raising Professionals—past local chapter president
  - American Society of Association Executives—on the board of allied group
- Career Training:
  - Various management courses
  - Number of fundraising courses
- Certifications:
  - Certified Association Executive
  - Certified Fund Raising Executive
- Outside interests:
  - A Big Brother
  - Enjoys outdoor sports including hunting, fishing, and boating

Ralph is a member of several support organizations in the not-for-profit field. He has kept on the cutting edge through various training opportunities as well as earning two industry certifications. His outside interests include volunteering and recreational pursuits. This fact illustrates that he practices what he preaches and that he has found a way to relieve stress from his very active life.

Ralph has been the CEO of Youth Center for 7 years and has been with the organization for a total of 12 years. He feels that his work is a calling, and he enjoys making a difference in the lives of the youth he serves. His board and his staff know and appreciate his dedication and work ethic.

Ralph is 51 years old. Although he is confident that the volunteer leadership would support him if he wished to stay until he retires, he feels that perhaps he could do even more good if he sought a CEO position in a national youth-serving organization.

Since Ralph has not been approached by another not-for-profit to be a candidate for a CEO position, he will need to test the waters by starting the process himself. Ralph decided to take a closer look at his possibilities. He used his research skills to determine if now is the right time for him to search for a new position. Exhibit 2.7 provides the results of his research. A blank self-evaluator form can be found on the CD-ROM that accompanies this text.

To fully analyze his potential opportunities, Ralph asked himself six questions to determine if he wanted to pursue a new CEO position in a not-for-profit:

1. Would leaving my current CEO position be the right move for me?
2. If I decide to conduct a search, what kind of CEO role will I seek?
3. What are the minimum standards that I seek in a new CEO position?
4. What skills can I emphasize to persuade the leadership of a prospective not-for-profit that I am the right person for the position?
5. Do I need to acquire any new skills before I seek a new position?
6. Will the new CEO position be my final career move or merely a stepping-stone to other opportunities?

Question 1: Would Leaving My Current CEO Position Be the Right Move for Me? Ralph realizes that he must answer this question. If he did not like his current position, the answer would be easy; but Ralph really enjoys being the CEO of Youth Center, Inc. He feels that leaving his current position will be a tough decision, but he also knows it might be the right move for both him and his organization. After he conducts his review, Ralph may very well find that he wants to stay with his current position. Even so, the process will have been beneficial.

Ralph began to analyze this question.

- Ralph feels that he has accomplished most or all of what he had set out to achieve in his current position. He has stabilized the financial operations, he has significantly

EXHIBIT 2.7   THE NOT-FOR-PROFIT CEO POSITION
SELF-EVALUATOR FOR CURRENT CEOS

Name: *Ralph Moore*   Date completed: *M/D/Y*

1. Would leaving my current CEO position be the right move for me?
   - *I have accomplished most if not all of what I had set out to achieve.*
   - *I am running out of ideas in my current position.*
   - *I am getting bored at times doing the same activities.*
   - *I feel that I have the energy to assume at least one new CEO position in a not-for-profit.*
   - *I think I could handle leaving my current position.*

2. If I decide to conduct a search, what CEO role will I seek?
   - *What do I seek in a new position?*
   - *What kind of organization do I ideally seek?*
   - *What kind of organization would I not seek?*
   - *To what geographical area would I limit my move?*

3. What are the minimum standards that I seek in a new CEO position?
   - *What is the governance structure that I desire?*
   - *What size organization would I seek?*
   - *Would the fiscal health of the organization be a factor?*
   - *Would the reputation of the organization matter?*

4. What skills can I emphasize to persuade the leadership of a prospective not-for-profit that I am the right person for the position?
   - *How can I emphasize my unique skills?*
   - *What kind of practical methods can I use to educate the key people?*

5. Do I need to acquire any additional skills before I seek a new position?
   - *Do I have sufficient academic skills?*
   - *What additional training will I need?*

6. Will the new CEO position be my final career move or merely a stepping-stone to other opportunities?
   - *How many CEO positions do I wish to assume for the rest of my career?*
   - *What is my long-term plan to fulfill that goal?*

---

increased the reserves, and he even started an endowment fund. Ralph conducted a successful capital campaign to fund the new youth center. Membership is up and, through his leadership, he has attracted a very strong board. Although he still feels like he has more to accomplish, the items remaining on the plate are minor.

- Ralph is known as an ideas person. Although many of his ideas have been implemented successfully, lately new ideas are getting harder to discover.

- Ralph loves his job, but some of the activities that the organization conducts annually are beginning to bore him. From time to time, he will find excuses to be doing other business so he will not have to attend.
- Ralph feels like he has bottled up energy that is not being used at the organization. He finds himself using this energy as a volunteer for other organizations or for his outside interests. He wonders if he can use this energy in another position.

In the end, Ralph is starting to realize that, if the right position came along, he would be able to handle leaving his current CEO post.

Question 2: If I Decide to Conduct a Search, What CEO Role Will I Seek?

After evaluating his current situation and his long-term career goals, Ralph has decided to conduct a job search. He realizes that his search will take time, but he is comfortable with that because he is determined to find as perfect a position as possible.

To start the process, Ralph has listed the reasons why he is seeking a new position:

- To increase his capacity to serve
- To find a position at the national level where he can make a difference
- To be recognized on the national level
- To find greater opportunities to give back to the not-for-profit community
- To receive additional compensation
- To have enough income to increase his savings for retirement

These reasons will serve Ralph well as he begins his search. Such a list is very important, but it must be an honest summary of why you are seeking a new CEO position. The list will help you identify why you feel the urge to leave your current CEO position for another. Through this process, you can determine the types of organizations that appeal to you and, perhaps more important, the kinds of organizations that do not.

The kind of organization you wish to seek is perhaps the most important decision you will make. In Ralph's case, he wises to seek a CEO position in a national youth-related organization. Most of his career positions were related to youth-serving organizations and that is what he is accustomed to.

Yet Ralph did have one career position with Community Services, Inc., an organization dealing with family social services issues. Ralph was not as fond of the wider role that the organization played even though youth were a major part of the equation. With this experience, Ralph has wisely determined to be flexible in the type of organizations he seeks at this time. After all, the timing and opportunities for CEO positions can be sparse.

On the other hand, Ralph has also focused on the types of organizations he does not wish to seek. He does not feel well suited for a CEO position in a trade association or professional society. Although Ralph can keep his options open, he is determined to start his initial search with these parameters.

Ralph has also decided to limit his search by geography. He would entertain any possibility, but he feels that this will help him to focus his search. Ralph lives in Richmond, Virginia, and he enjoys the area. His family all live within 200 miles so he has decided to limit his search to a 300-mile radius from his current location.

Question 3: What Are the Minimum Standards That I Seek in a New CEO Position?   Ralph is fairly rigid in this area and wisely so. His background and his knowledge of other CEOs' situations have taught him that the organization that he wishes to lead must meet minimum standards. Ralph's primary concern is the governance structure of each potential organization.

He will be able to discover a lot of information about the governance structure of potential organizations through online searches and printed materials. He will be looking to avoid troubled organizations—ones that are top-heavy with too many board members or ones where the CEO seems to report to more than one officer. A general search may also provide information on the number of board meetings per year, how extensive the volunteer committee structure may be, and how the staff relates to volunteers and the CEO.

The important questions, however, are more difficult to determine through this process; such questions include, for example, how the balance of power is distributed between the board and the CEO. Although this can mean the success or failure of a new CEO if he or she does not have the power to lead, often it is not documented or discussed during the search process unless the incumbent CEO engineers an opportunity to address it. Ralph is determined to bring the balance-of-power question up with each potential organization early in his search process.

The question about organization size often comes up in a search profile standard. At first, Ralph got caught up with the idea that he wanted to lead an organization with a larger budget, more staff, and a greater volunteer structure. He soon realized that he was looking at his search from the wrong perspective.

Although ample resources are needed to fulfill any mission, Ralph is aware of several organizations that have huge budgets and hundreds of staff and volunteers yet they never seem to truly address their missions or make a difference. The leaders of these organizations spend most of their time dealing with keeping the ship afloat, attending endless meetings, and traveling on public relations junkets. These organizations' brands are well known, but Ralph questioned whether holding the CEO position at such organizations would be enjoyable and if their governance structure would encourage the CEO to use his imagination.

As far as compensation goes, Ralph has long ago determined it is not the number-one concern in his career. In the past, he decided to pursue opportunities where he could make a difference. He is determined to search for a position that fulfills that goal this time around, too.

Ralph knows that the fiscal health of the prospective organization is a key factor. He has a solid background in understanding the kinds of fiscal systems and controls that should be in place to administer and safeguard an operation. He is also a seasoned fundraiser.

Ralph is realistic in his search; he knows that he may find a not-for-profit that has everything he desires, yet he is willing to consider an organization with the potential to be brought up to speed. He knows that the key to such a turnaround would be based on:

- The partnership/governance structure in place
- The current volunteer leadership
- The staff assigned to finance and fundraising functions
- Most important, the potential for expanding income streams

Ralph is determined to obtain detailed information on each prospective not-for-profit organization's fiscal integrity online, through hardcopy materials, and by asking search committees.

Ralph wants to make sure that he will become the CEO of a reputable organization. He is not concerned if the organization has adversaries; he knows the ones that really make the difference often do. He also knows that such adversaries usually come from two points of view:

1. Individuals and organizations that are at the opposite end of the spectrum; those squarely set against the mission of the organization
2. Organizations (and often the individuals within them) with the same basic interests that see the not-for-profit in question as a competitor, have personality conflicts with key players, or even are jealous of what the organization has accomplished

Ralph knows that handling adversity is a part of the job and he can handle it. What he wants to make sure of, however, is that a prospective organization does not have an insurmountable obstacle, such as a scandal that would take years to overcome and would take him away from fulfilling the mission of the organization.

Question 4: What Skills Can I Emphasize to Persuade the Leadership of a Prospective Not-for-Profit That I Am the Right Person for the Position?
Ralph knows that he has a number of the skills needed to address most challenges faced by today's not-for-profits. He is also aware that he will have to tailor his approach to each prospective not-for-profit that he pursues. Ralph knows that he will need to emphasize certain unique skills over others based on his analysis of what each prospective organization needs the most.

If Ralph seeks a youth education–based not-for-profit that needs a strong administrator and someone who can increase the organization's capacity, for example, he can emphasize his academic work, professional certifications, and any published work. In addition, he can provide examples of how he has refined his current operation to better serve its mission. He should also let the search committee know that capacity building starts with significantly increasing funding, which is another one of his skills.

Educating search committees and boards of directors starts with a cover letter, resume, or curriculum vitae. Yet, you should never miss the opportunity to educate anyone in the organization at any step in the process. This includes telephone calls, e-mails, letters, and in-person encounters. Your message needs to be clear, focused, simple, and direct. If Ralph seeks a youth education–based not-for-profit, his core message may be:

> I am seeking the CEO position of this organization to fulfill a personal career goal that I am passionate about as well as to ensure that the important work it performs can be provided to those who need it.
>
> I am confident that I can fulfill this role based on my academic background, by keeping on the cutting edge through ongoing training, and by renewing my certifications. I also bring an extensive background in not-for-profit administration and fund procurement to the table that will help maintain the integrity of your organization and assist in significantly increasing its capacity.
>
> I am thrilled to be a candidate. I firmly believe that my academic and career pursuits have prepared me for this important assignment.

Question 5: Do I Need to Acquire Any Additional Skills Before I Seek a New Position?   Like most of us who have been around for a while, Ralph thought he was fine in this category. After all, he had earned a doctorate degree, which he knew could set him apart in a number of searches. As the National Study of Not-for-Profit CEOs discovered, nearly 66 percent of the participating CEOs held graduate degrees while 16 percent held doctorate degrees. Details of this study can be found in the companion book to this workbook. Ralph knows that search committees seek CEOs with higher degrees.

Although Ralph has kept up with the latest management techniques and technology through local and national training, he began to think that he might want to take courses in negotiations and persuasion techniques. He also thought that a class or two on message enhancement might serve him as well. Ralph is wise to pursue these classes to gain additional skills. Anyone who seeks a new opportunity must be up to speed—it is often the small differences between you and another candidate that can enhance your chances.

Question 6: Will the New CEO Position Be My Final Career Move or Merely a Stepping-Stone to Other Opportunities?   Ralph is not really sure how to answer this question. His next move could very well be his last CEO position; Ralph would like it if that were the case. However, due to his age and the average tenure of a not-for-profit CEO, Ralph feels that he needs to prepare for both possibilities.

From his research, he knows that the number of CEO positions held by each individual over a career depends on a variety of variables.

Among the CEOs who participated in the National Study of Not-for-Profit CEOs, 46.53 percent had held only one CEO position. Another 47.53 percent had held two to six CEO positions over the course of their career. Of this group, 28.71 percent had held two positions and 13.87 percent had held three positions.

Ralph has 14 years left in his career life. He is wisely considering the possibility of additional CEO positions beyond his current search. He knows that this means two things:

1. If he finds a new CEO position, he will need to work hard and think long term, as if he will be there for his entire career, because he just might be.

2. At the same time, he will need to continue to build his network and to refine his personal skills with an eye toward potential future opportunities.

Ralph knows that taking such a course will not be easy; it will require developing a long-term plan to detail each step that he needs to make. He has recalled the advice that one of his mentors gave him early in his career:

> The best way to have people seek you out to do greater things is to do great things in the position that you hold right now.

Over the years, Ralph realized that this was pretty good advice. In many ways, the advice got him his present position and certainly will be a help for the rest of his career. At the same time, Ralph is aware that he must sell himself. Looking back at his career, Ralph recognized that most of his advancement opportunities were accomplished through an orchestrated blend of successful work and self-promotion. Ralph feels that his self-evaluation will provide an excellent base for developing a successful search for his next CEO position.

SUMMARY

From the minute an individual enters the work field, something interesting happens. Each of us determines, for the most part subconsciously, how we will approach our job. Some will determine that it is a way to make money, some will look upon the task as a step to power, while others will look at what they are doing as a calling. Even though most individuals could make the argument that all three viewpoints define their career to some extent, usually one of these tendencies is dominant.

My wife, Sue, and I recently had dinner with a couple in their 40s who both had careers in the health field. As they talked about their careers, you could see and hear their enthusiasm and excitement about what they were doing. It was obvious that they had a calling. Yet they also had powerful positions that earned a decent amount of money. They were wise to enter a field of work that was a calling because their enthusiasm brought them success; the money and power issues often fall into place when you are successful.

From the examples of Frank Fulton, Janet McGuire, and Ralph Moore, we cannot really tell if they feel what they are doing is a calling or not. If they actually existed and you could talk with them, you might be able to tell their level of enthusiasm. The examples are like paper cut-outs. A lot of individuals go through their careers like paper cut-outs, lacking any kind of enthusiasm and just going through the motions. Individuals who do not seek positions that are a calling are missing out on a tremendous high, and it is one of the most important keys to success.

The Process of Getting Things Done

The greatest thing in this world is not so much where we are, but in which direction we are moving.

—Oliver Wendell Holmes

INTRODUCTION

Being successful at getting things done is an art that can be applied at any level. It is the major key to being successful in the tasks that you are currently doing, and it creates a sound foundation for the building blocks for your future. The National Study of Not-for-Profit CEOs revealed that past experiences rank as the highest reason for why CEOs attained their positions.

For those in the field, this comes as no surprise. What was surprising, however, was how much higher it ranked compared to other measures of success. Exhibit 3.1 shows that "past experiences" ranked as the number-one factor, at 69.30 percent, as compared to "networking," at only 11.88 percent. Although any CEO would tell you that there are a number of factors that will affect your success, the participating CEOs made it absolutely clear that past experience is the key factor to attaining the corner office.

The companion book to this workbook explains how individuals at any stage in their career can attain and retain a CEO position. Chapter 2 details how to secure the top position. Chapter 3 illustrates that retaining a CEO position is actually far more challenging than obtaining the position in the first place. Chapter 5 provides survival techniques for attaining and retaining a CEO position.

This section of the workbook complements the book by highlighting the tools for "Getting Things Done." Best of all, the information provided is based on the actual experiences of the over 100 CEOs who participated in the study.

EXHIBIT 3.1	HOW PARTICIPATING CEOS RANKED WHY THEY ATTAINED THEIR CURRENT POSITIONS
Past experiences	69.30%
Networking	11.88%
Formal education	10.89%
Other	3.97%
Ongoing training	1.98%
Certifications	1.98%
Total	**100%**

THE REALITY FACTOR

The first thing that you must realize is that the tools to help you to attain the corner office—*The Not-for-Profit CEO,* this workbook, mentors, formal and ongoing education, certification opportunities, and even past experience—are not worth anything unless you really want to:

- Take calculated risks
- Apply all these factors to design a career plan
- Become a CEO

No one has ever earned anything worthwhile in life without taking at least one or more calculated risks. Note that I said *calculated* risks. That means, for example, making a key point or advising a supervisor that you have a better way or idea to accomplish a task. It may also mean being willing to do something that is not listed in your job description but will enhance your employer in some way. Each time you take a calculated risk, you demonstrate leadership and worth. You also get noticed more, and eventually it may even result in being offered a better position.

I began by taking calculated risks early in my career. One of the first risks that I remember taking was when I discovered that a new department was being formed within the organization in which I worked. This new department had an exciting mission that I thought would be an ideal fit for me. I was also aware that a position in this department could provide me with the visibility I needed to advance to other opportunities.

This new department was in charge of developing career programs for high school students. At the time, I was assigned to work on youth programs for much younger children. Although I enjoyed this work, I did not want to miss out on a new opportunity. So I simply acted on my own and organized three high school programs in my territory and made sure that they were running well before I announced their formation at a full staff meeting. I turned the paperwork over to the director of teen programs, who received credit for the new business, and I went about my old role for the next six months.

One day my supervisor called me into his office and announced that the director of the teen program had been moved to another position and that they wanted me to take over the program. In the promotion announcement, my employer mentioned that I was chosen for this position due to the unselfish role I played in forming three teenage programs in my territory. Taking calculated risks on your way to the corner office is part of the game.

Everyone designs a career plan for themselves in some way. The process begins early in life as we begin to eliminate choices. We tend to concentrate on what we like to do or what we feel are the skills that come most easy to us. It is an awkward process that has a number of flaws.

During these early stages, it is much easier to focus on what you like to do rather than on the skills you think you may or may not have. When I was young, I hated onions. By the time I reached my late teens, I could not eat enough of them, and I still feel the same today.

Many CEOs tell me that the skills they enjoy the most were ones they acquired early in life, such as the art of dealing with people, but that those skills were the last things they thought would be their key to their success. Other CEOs were shy and inward individuals as young people and had to work hard on being more outgoing to accomplish what they wanted in life. Almost all of the participants in the National Study of Not-for-Profit CEOs worked very hard at refining their skills as well as developing a personal plan for success in their careers.

Not everyone thinks this way, however. Many people simply seem to let outside forces do the planning for them. This is particularly true of the path that they take throughout their careers. They are not in control of their careers; rather, they wait for someone to come along to grant them the big promotion.

Letting others control your career path is a huge mistake. No one is more interested in your career than you are. Therefore, who should be in charge? Never let anyone else take this role away from you.

Repeat after me:

I, _____ (insert full name), am the chief executive officer of _____ (insert last name), Inc.

Once you comprehend this core fact, you will never be unemployed again even if you are between jobs.

In my book *The Not-for-Profit CEO: How to Attain & Retain the Corner Office,* I devote a lot of space to the question: Do you really want to become a CEO? Prospective candidates need to ask themselves this important question often. There is only one CEO position available in a not-for-profit, so few are chosen.

Ask yourself: If, for some reason, you never become a CEO, what would be your fallback career path? Many people determine that the sacrifices of attaining and retaining the corner office are not worth it, and that is all right. It is never too late to change your course if the CEO position is not suited for you.

It is not all right, however, if you did not attain the position simply because you did not understand the process. There are three secrets to success for CEOs:

1. They know how to attain the position.
2. They really enjoy the role.
3. They are willing to put in the time and the energy needed to retain the position.

THE PLANNING PROCESS

Section 4, The Career Strategic Planner, details the process that you can use to plan your career. This section also provides a few ideas on how to implement the process of getting things done at various stages of a career. These are the building blocks for developing a successful career strategic plan.

High School Students

Although some of the CEOs who participated in the study knew that they wanted to pursue careers in the not-for-profit community early in life, most did not. In fact, most of the CEOs indicated that they were unaware of career opportunities in this sector until much later in life.

Today, there is a much greater awareness of not-for-profit careers in general, even among high school students. More than ever, young adults are seeking careers that can provide a service to others. High school students who have begun to take charge of their lives are seeking information on a number of opportunities much earlier than past generations. In fact, one of the major goals of every student should be to gain as much career information as possible during the high school years. It is a great time to discover what is out there and what may match your interests and talents.

The Self-Assessment Tool for High School Students is a good starting point for organizing information about yourself and a good place to begin to develop your Career Strategic Planner. Exhibit 3.2 presents a completed self-assessment tool for Theresa Rodriguez. A blank form for your use can be found on the CD-ROM that accompanies this workbook.

Theresa has some interest in local community organization work, but, as you can see, she has a lot of other interests, as well. At her age, this is normal. The self-evaluation will help her to clarify, at least for now, what careers she might be interested in. Although this may change several times over her

EXHIBIT 3.2	SELF-ASSESSMENT TOOL FOR HIGH SCHOOL STUDENTS

Name: _Theresa Rodriguez_   Date completed: _M/D/Y_

1. The three subjects that I like the best in school:

Subjects	Chief Reason Why
a. *History*	*Enjoy discovering how we build on the past*
b. *Economics*	*Plays a major role in our lives*
c. *English*	*Language skills are a key to the past*

2. The three subjects that I like the least in school:

Subjects	Chief Reason Why
a. *Health*	*Seems to be the same thing all of the time*
b. *Literature*	*I get bored with learning the material*
c. *Physical fitness*	*I like to exercise on my own*

3. The extracurricular activities that I like the best:

   a. *Debating Club*
   b. *Women's track team*
   c. *Class politics*

4. These are the nonschool activities that I participate in and ranked based on which ones I enjoy the most (1 being the one I most enjoy):

Activities	Rank
a. *Church-sponsored teen program*	*1*
b. *Part-time job*	*2*

5. The top career choices that I have made at this point and my chief reason why I chose them:

Career Choices	Chief Reason Why	Rank
a. *History teacher*	*Enjoy subject*	*4*
b. *Journalist*	*Be able to report the news*	*3*
c. *Coach*	*Enjoy team programs*	*1*
d. *Lawyer*	*Like to win arguments*	*5*
e. *Activities director*	*Want to work to help people*	*2*

6. A listing of the career areas that I am not interested in at this time and the chief reason why (1 being the career area that I would least like to work in):

Career Choices	Chief Reason Why	Rank
a. *Politician*	*Want a long-term career*	*5*
b. *Scientist*	*Feel I do not have the skills*	*4*
c. *Doctor*	*I do not like to be around sick people*	*3*
d. *Accountant*	*The job seems boring to me*	*1*
e. *Retailing*	*The hours and being at one location*	*2*

(continues)

EXHIBIT 3.2   SELF-ASSESSMENT TOOL FOR HIGH SCHOOL STUDENTS *(Continued)*

7. Am I planning to investigate the opportunities that I currently have selected for future career choices? ___Yes___ (Yes/No). If I answered yes, what is my plan?

   Please review my plan in Section 4: The Career Strategic Planner.

8. To date who have I asked to help me investigate future careers?

   Parents: ___Yes___

   Teachers: ___Yes___   If so, who: *Janet Simpson, my English teacher*

   Others: ___Yes___   If so, who: *Jim Thompson, my debating club coach*

9. What are the requirements of the career areas that interest me?

Career Areas	Education	Experience
a. *History teacher*	*BA/MS degrees*	*Teacher certificate*
b. *Journalist*	*BA degree*	*Writing*
c. *Coach*	*BA degree*	*Coaching*
d. *Lawyer*	*JD degree*	*Clerking, etc.*
e. *Activities director*	*BA degree*	*Organizing people*

10. What other information can I provide that will help me to develop my Career Strategic Plan?

    I enjoy working with people, I want to find a position where I can give something back to the community, a job that I would enjoy doing every day.

Signature: *Theresa Rodriguez*

---

high school years, the self-evaluation will help her through this process by eliminating career choices that are not a good fit and discovering new choices that may be an even better fit.

Please note that the self-assessment focuses on course work that Theresa likes and dislikes. Of the courses she is taking, Theresa likes history, economics, and English but is not so fond of health, literature, or physical education.

The reasons why she likes or dislikes these subjects are really what is most revealing. Theresa seems to have a very good understanding of why we study history and why economics is so important. She is aware that there is a very practical reason why English is taught. As far as health, literature, and physical education go, Theresa finds the first two to be boring and last one to be a waste of time because she is already doing similar exercises through extracurricular sports.

Obviously, Theresa needs to focus on all of her subjects. However, like most of us, she has favorites that she likes or excels in. For a career planning purposes, this is very valuable information.

Theresa's extracurricular activities reveal additional areas of interest. The debate club reveals that she may have negotiation skills or the ability change or refine opinions. The women's track team shows she enjoys physical activity and demonstrates a strong desire to win. Her interest in class politics offers the hope that Theresa may have leadership skills.

Theresa's nonschool activities illustrate that she has a wholesome social life and that she has some core religious beliefs. Religious beliefs, incidentally, seemed to be one of the key success factors that participating CEOs noted in the CEO study. Theresa's part-time job also indicates that she is willing to do her part to meet family needs or to offset future educational costs.

Theresa's list of preferred career choices provides good data on her current thinking. Like most young people, her list will change over time, but it provides a starting point to investigate these careers and to begin to eliminate those that do not measure up to her satisfaction. Her career choices vary a great deal, yet there is a common theme to all of them. For the purposes of evaluation, the most important information is the chief reason why Theresa chose these careers:

Chief Reasons Why	Rank
Enjoy the subject	4
Be able to report the news	3
Enjoy team sports	1
Like to win an argument	5
Want to work to help people	2

These statements provide a peek at what Theresa may seek in her future career. She wants to enjoy her work and to be involved with a position that is timely and up to date. She also wants to be part of a team and may be interested in a profession that influences people. Theresa also wants a career where she can help others. The ranking is important too: teamwork is one, helping others is two, and a timely position is three.

The career areas that do not interest Theresa can also help to focus her search. Once again, the chief reasons why she does not want certain careers is the most important part:

Chief Reasons Why	Rank
Want a long-term career, not just a job	5
Feel I do not have the skills	4
Do not want to be around sick people	3
Job seems boring	1
Hours and being at one location	2

Theresa wants a position with meaning, not just a job. It is important to her to have the skills needed to perform that job and to be successful. In addition, she wants to work in an uplifting job environment that is stimulating and has regular hours. In a nutshell, Theresa wants a position that is enjoyable and that fits into her future lifestyle.

The self-assessment also asked Theresa if she had a plan to help guide her career as well as a plan to investigate the opportunities that she has chosen as possible career choices. Theresa does have a plan, which will be revealed in Section 4.

It is important that Theresa and other high school students have adult support as they begin to investigate career opportunities. Parents should be the number-one support mechanism, but other people are needed as well. These individuals can range from school counselors to others who can perform a greater role as advisors and mentors. It is important that these individuals agree to stay involved throughout the process to help young people make sound decisions and prepare them for future careers. At the moment, Theresa has two teachers who are helping her.

The companion book takes an in-depth look at the vital role that mentors played in the career success of the CEOs who participated in the national survey.

The next question on the self-assessment concerns educational requirements. Theresa recognizes that advanced education will be needed for all the positions that she is investigating. The minimum education required can run from an undergraduate degree to a doctorate. She also recognizes that most of her career choices will require some experience prior to assuming the ideal position. This may mean that Theresa will need on-the-job training ranging from internships to earning certifications.

The final question is purposely open-ended. Theresa has let us know that she wants to work with people and that she wants a job that gives back to the community. She also wants a job that will be enjoyable. This sounds like a tall order but, with proper planning, Theresa can achieve all of this and more.

Upon reflection, Theresa has selected these careers as her top positions to seek:

- Coaching
- Activities director
- Journalist

There is a better than even chance that Theresa will never assume any of these positions. However, the search and the in-depth investigation of these and other positions will point her in the right direction. She will need to continue to adapt her plan to fit new and emerging thoughts.

College Students

Once an individual makes a commitment to attend college, he or she has at least begun to focus on a general career area. In most cases, however, these choices will be refined and, in some cases, significantly changed while still in school. This is a healthy process that allows the individual to test the waters while there is still time to make a change.

The college experience is both a wonderful and a scary process. On the plus side, for many, it is the first time in their lives that they are on their own and get to make both everyday and life-changing decisions. The scary part is that these decisions can have a profound affect on their lives.

Of course, one of the major decisions is career choice. This is the reason why most people enter college in the first place—although college students may need to remind themselves of this fact from time to time. Career choice is a very personal thing. Even if you have friends who are majoring in the same discipline, chances are that they do not have the same career ambitions that you do.

This workbook is designed to help individuals interested in careers in the not-for-profit arena and, in particular, those who aspire to become CEOs. However, the career planning process should also involve exploration into what individuals want to do with their lives. Perhaps this workbook will inspire you to go forward to pursue a career in the not-for-profit field—or it might reveal that such a career is not for you. Either way, the process has been useful.

I encourage you to adapt the process to fit your needs by using the workbook and the forms from the CD-ROM.

Exhibit 3.3 can assist college students in making an educated decision on a possible career in the not-for-profit field. Lewis Johnston has already filled out this form. A blank form can be found on the CD-ROM.

Lewis is a typical college student who is trying to make it through school. His challenges include working part time to help pay for his education as well as trying to nail down his career choice. He may find his way soon, and he may gradually drift toward a general area. Like many, he may spend his entire college career searching.

The self-assessment tool is designed to help college students begin the discovery process rather than make an instant decision. As Lewis's self-assessment notes, he is still looking at several careers. This is healthy. His college experience has just begun, and he has taken only a few courses in his major.

Lewis currently is looking at three career choices. Many other college students might list more choices; that all right. The actual reasons why Lewis chose these careers is what is really important. His reasons reveal why he favors these choices and may shed light on what he is seeking in a career choice overall.

Lewis has stated his desire to have a career related to his educational background, to be involved in exciting work, and to seek a career that makes a difference. All of these are logical expectations and worthy goals. His current major and minor fit well also.

Lewis has taken three courses in his major and has done fairly well. His comfort zone varies, however, and accounting seems to be an area that he may want to pursue.

EXHIBIT 3.3   SELF-ASSESSMENT TOOL FOR COLLEGE STUDENTS

Name: *Lewis Johnston*   Date completed: *M/D/Y*

1. What are my current career choices?

Career Choices	Why
For-profit management	*Current degree program*
Sales/marketing	*Seems like an exciting area*
Not-for-profit management	*To be involved, to make a difference*

2. My current major/minor:

   Major: *Business Administration*

   Minor: *Accounting*

3. Courses in my current major that I have taken:

Courses	Final Grade	Comfort Zone (1 to 10, 1 being the highest)
Introduction to Business	*B*	*2*
Accounting I	*B−*	*5*
Computer Tech.	*B*	*3*

4. The nonmajor courses I have taken to date that I liked:

Courses	Why I Liked Them
Speech	*Enjoy speaking in front of people*
American History	*I like to imagine how past generations lived*
Spanish	*I feel the ability of speaking another language would be an asset*

5. The courses I have taken to date that I disliked:

Courses	Why I Disliked Them
Biology	*I do not like to memorize terms*
English Literature	*Boring*
Introduction to Math	*Not my best subject*

6. What I seek in a career, ranking the top five (1 being the top reason):

	Rank
a. *I want to like what I do.*	*2*
b. *I want to make a difference.*	*4*
c. *It must be an area in which I can advance.*	*3*
d. *I want a position that has a professional status.*	*5*
e. *The position needs to provide enough compensation for me to provide for my family.*	*1*

THE PLANNING PROCESS **51**

EXHIBIT 3.3 SELF-ASSESSMENT TOOL FOR COLLEGE
STUDENTS (Continued)

7. The educational credentials I seek:
   a. *A BS degree in Business Administration*
   b. *Perhaps a master's degree in a few years*

8. The noneducational activities that I participate in:

Activities	Why
I am on the baseball team	*Enjoy the sport and team effort*
Community Service Club	*I like to help others*
ROTC	*Helps me pay for college and has some leadership training as well*

9. Do I volunteer? ___*Yes*___ (Yes/no); if yes, please answer the following questions:

   Volunteer for what organization: *PAL Program*
   What do I do: *I coach and counsel kids.*
   Number of hours a month: *About 20 hours*
   Why I volunteer: *It is a great program, it helped me.*
   What I gain from the experience: *I get as much out of it as I give.*

10. If I chose to work for a not-for-profit someday, would I aspire to become a CEO?
    ___*Yes*___ (Yes/no); if yes, why?

    I am not sure what it takes to work full time for a not-for-profit or to be a CEO, but I know that when I am volunteering, I see the good work that the PAL program does and find myself wondering if I could be happy working for such an organization. I also like to lead. I am the squad leader on my baseball team and enjoy being a coach. I feel that if I become a not-for-profit professional someday I would want to lead the organization.

The elective courses that he has taken reveal some strong points for Lewis, including public speaking, the use of his imagination, and a desire to speak another language. These strengths will provide a sound base for the positions that he is investigating.

Lewis has also indicated the classes that he dislikes, which may reveal a weak area or two. For example, math and science may not be the ideal areas for him to pursue. This is good to know early in college. As far as English literature is concerned, Lewis feels that it is just a boring subject.

Lewis has also provided a logical array of reasons for what he seeks in a career. He wants a position that he will enjoy day in and day out. This is very reasonable, and it is one of the primary reasons that a person plans a career in the first place. In my career, I have held a couple of positions that I did not like, and going to work was pure torture. No one should have to endure that.

Lewis also wants to make a difference in his job. Such a situation can be a bit more difficult to find. Both the for-profit and not-for-profit sectors offer such positions, but you need to investigate ahead of time to know for sure. In addition, Lewis wants a career where he can advance to the top. This is something that should be investigated every time an individual seeks a new position. Lewis also wants a position that has professional status. A number of positions can provide status, including many in the not-for-profit sector.

Compensation is a factor for Lewis. He wants to be sure that he has enough money to live on. This is a challenge as you embark on and land that first position. Although it is important, it should not be a primary factor for choosing a position. Generally speaking, if you are happy with your current work, you will tend to advance at a quicker pace. During my career, I have witnessed several talented people "go for the money" with no thought about the position itself. All this yields is a miserable life. I am convinced that these individuals are not as successful as they would have been, including in the area of compensation, had they sought positions that really appealed to them.

Lewis is seeking an undergraduate degree that will be a good start for his career. Ultimately, he is also considering earning a master's degree. This is a wise decision, particularly if he wishes to aspire to become a CEO. Over 65 percent of those who participated in the National Study of Not-for-Profit CEOs had earned graduate degrees.

It is interesting to hear what Lewis has to say about his noneducational activities. He is on the baseball team at college for his love for the sport as well as for the involvement in the team effort. It sounds like a valuable experience. He notes that his role in the Community Services Club is due to his desire to help others. His participation in ROTC helped him to pay for college as well as providing leadership training. Lewis is beginning to establish a solid and varied background that will pay him dividends later in life.

Lewis also volunteers at the PAL program, where he coaches and counsels youngsters. When asked why he volunteers, he said that he believes in the activity and that the PAL program helped him personally. Lewis is already learning the valuable lesson that giving back to others is the right and proper thing to do. He also realizes that he is gaining as much from the experience as he is giving. Lewis is wise beyond his years.

I empirically documented this "return benefits" factor in a study showing the benefits volunteers receive from the act of helping others. Chief among the return benefits of volunteering is acquiring leadership traits. The details of this study can be found in my book *The Universal Benefits of Volunteering,* published by John Wiley & Sons.

Lewis has stated that he would like to become a CEO if he seeks a professional career in the not-for-profit community. He feels that he is a natural leader and that he has gained insight into this role through several experiences both at school and in the community.

Lewis Johnston seems to have the desire and the raw talent to make a successful drive for the corner office. It will not be easy, but, if he can develop a well-tuned Career Strategic Plan, he might just make it. To find out how to create such a plan, see Section 4.

Professionals in the Field

I can still recall my first day of work in my first not-for-profit position. I had just graduated from college and had accepted a position roughly 100 miles away from my hometown of Philadelphia. I reported to work in the only suit I owned and barely made it into work because my car was on its last legs. Although I did not realize it at the time, the CEO of this organization was one of the best in the field.

Until this point, I had spent my summers away from home working. My college was over 400 miles from home. Yet I felt a strange sense of loneliness on my first day. I did not know anyone in the area. I would soon be meeting other coworkers and I knew that I would be dealing with hundreds of volunteers and thousands of members who would rely on me to serve them.

My CEO, a very unorthodox leader, sensed my trepidation and put me at ease immediately. He was a master at reading people, and, more importantly, he knew how to use this skill to get people to do things that they never thought were possible. In my case, this was being able to take on the role of a professional not-for-profit executive. Thus began my professional career with the Boy Scouts of America as a district executive of a territory spanning half of a county.

This position provided me with a great base as it required nearly all of the skills a successful CEO would need. I advised a district committee that resembled a board, I supported volunteer commissioners who oversaw the program aspects of the district, and I was required to raise funds including major gifts, sponsorships, and small individual donations. I had a membership goal, I was the chief spokesperson of my territory, and I was a meeting planner organizing banquets and major outings that involved nearly 1,000 attendees. I was even required to write and publish a monthly newsletter. Today, I still use the skills acquired during my first professional assignment.

Although I did well in this environment, in some ways I was not really ready for it. I was 22 years old but looked much younger, which became a source of teasing by the professional staff and even some volunteers. I knew down deep that I wanted to become a professional not-for-profit leader, but I knew that I needed to learn my craft and mature some more.

About a year after I started this position, Uncle Sam sent me a telegram and required me to be involved with another kind of opportunity. Even though I was not happy to be diverted from my career and personal pursuits, in retrospect, it was the best thing that could have happened to me.

During my experience with the army, I gained a tremendous number of leadership skills and learned how to deal with people. I gained confidence in myself and, when I came home from Vietnam, I no longer looked like a boy. This experience also gave me a great deal of time to think about my future. I became determined to earn a graduate degree, and I even began taking courses while I was still in the service. While I was still in Vietnam, I applied for and was accepted to a graduate school in California.

I knew that I needed to have a job, so I applied for a not-for-profit position near the school. The day I was discharged in San Francisco, I traveled to Los Angeles, still in uniform, to interview for the not-for-profit position that I ended up securing.

Down deep, I knew that I wanted to devote my professional life to the not-for-profit community. I also knew that I wanted to become a leader. At the time, I did not fully understand what that meant, but I felt that I was heading in the right direction.

I knew that if I wanted to devote myself to this career area and that if I wanted to be a leader, someday I would need:

- Experience
- Formal educational credentials
- A way of keeping on the cutting edge
- A network of mentors and colleagues

Early in my career, I understood that experience was a primary factor in moving up the ladder. The CEOs who participated in the National Study of Not-for-Profit CEOs agreed with this statement. The overall majority indicated that the primary reason they were able to attain their current position was past experience. In fact, this answer towered over any other reason.

The need for past experience seemed obvious to me but, early on, I pondered the question of what constitutes past experience. The CEOs who participated in the study shed light on this area. Some felt that experience in one or two organizations was fine; others felt that experience in several organizations provided a more well-rounded background. Neither answer is necessarily correct—it depends mostly on the individual and his or her long-term goal.

Either way, the actual experiences that you have are the important factor; not the quantity of organizations you have been with. CEOs need to know the functions of the whole shop; not just a segment. They also need to know how to advance each and every part of the organization. In preparing to become a CEO, professionals need to develop a personal plan for gaining the diverse experience needed to run the entire show.

Education is a lifetime pursuit. As the CEOs who participated in the study demonstrated, advanced degrees are part of the credentials that search committees seek. Many, including me, earned their advance degrees while working full time.

You may think that this is impossible, but it can be done. A number of graduate schools offer programs that fit into professional career schedules. The American Society of Association Executives, for example, offers a doctoral degree program in association management through a partnership with the Union Institute and University. I am proud to say that I am one of the founders of that program.

Finding ways to keep on the cutting edge is vitally important for anyone who wishes to be successful in any career and is paramount for anyone who wishes to become a

CEO of a not-for-profit. Associations need to take advantage of every opportunity to be as effective as they can. These opportunities can come through the latest technology, management techniques, and other avenues.

In my shop, we never coast. We are constantly looking for new ways to do our jobs. Professionals in the field who wish to attain the CEO position need to think that way. You must constantly look for new ways to gain knowledge or new skills to enhance your current position and to prepare you for your future.

Building a network of mentors and colleagues is important for a successful career in any field. I cannot imagine not having such an asset. I have had hundreds of individuals in my network over the years. Some have stayed with me for a few years, some have drifted in and out, and others have been with me during my entire career.

One person who drifted in and out of my network was a college classmate. I happened to be his big brother in our fraternity. We saw each other throughout our college days but I cannot say that he was really a close friend at the time. I graduated a year before he did. After his graduation, he joined the same not-for-profit organization that I was employed by. Our paths crossed over the years, and we kept up on each other's career. From time to time, we consulted with each other, but often months or even years went by without contact.

About six years ago, I decided to develop a youth-based educational program for my current association, the U.S. Sportsmen's Alliance (USSA). I immediately thought that the perfect partner for this program would be the Boy Scouts of America (BSA). I called my friend, who had a key position at the BSA National Council to ask his advice and opinion. He provided me with sound advice and opened a few doors.

As a result of his help, the USSA has a successful youth educational program that partners with the Boy Scouts and other youth-serving organizations. The program serves thousands of young people in over 30 states. This anecdote makes it clear that networks are important to your career and vital to the success of a CEO. These relationships can last a lifetime.

Developing a plan of action is important if you want to be successful in your not-for-profit career and to become a leader in this field. Bear in mind that while you may receive help from others, no one is more interested in your career than you. You are the only one who can move the process along. To begin this process, you will need to do a self-assessment to discover:

- Your strengths and your weaknesses
- What you need to do to prepare

Exhibit 3.4 provides a good starting point. As you can see, Frank Fulton has illustrated how the form can be used. I encourage you to adapt the self-assessment tool for your personal use. A blank copy of the tool can be found on the CD-ROM that accompanies this workbook.

Frank is a seasoned not-for-profit executive who has served in three associations during his professional career of over 12 years. Like anyone, he has strengths and weaknesses. The self-assessment tool is designed to identify both traits.

Frank is very proud of his record of achievement in three professional positions, as well he should be. He was successful in all of them, and they have provided him with great experience including the ability to write, supervise staff, manage multiple tasks, and run a successful government affairs operation. It is important to measure your past experiences honestly. This self-assessment tool is for your own use; it is to your advantage to be as upfront with yourself as possible.

Frank has noted that there are several things he likes and few areas he dislikes about his current position as vice president of government affairs. He likes the ability and power to orchestrate change. It is one of his greatest thrills and one of the joys of being involved with not-for-profits.

EXHIBIT 3.4   SELF-ASSESSMENT TOOL FOR PROFESSIONALS IN THE FIELD

Name: _Frank Fulton_   Last completed: _M/D/Y_

1. These are the professional positions I have had to date:
   Position/Employer/Location: _____
   Description: _____
   Success Rate: _____   Satisfaction Rate: _____ (1 to 10, 1 being the highest)

   Assistant Director of Communications — Iowa Restaurant Association — Iowa
   Description: Supported the director and published the newsletter
   Success Rate: 2   Satisfaction Rate: 1

   Director of Field Services — Virginia Association of the Blind — Virginia
   Description: Managed the entire field operation, supervised 20
   Success Rate: 3   Satisfaction Rate: 2

   Vice President of Government Affairs — New Jersey Society of Home Growers
   Description: Lead the entire government affairs operation at both the state and federal level, supervised 10
   Success Rate: 2   Satisfaction Rate: 1

2. Here is a description of my current position:
   Title: _Vice President of Government Affairs_

  a. Experience level:
- Executive level: ___X___
- Middle management: _____
- Entry level: _____

  b. Number of individuals who report to me: ___10___

  c. Area that I work:
- Program: _____
- Administration: ___X___
- Other: _____

  d. Number of years that I have held this position: ___5___

  e. What I like the best about the position:
  The ability to orchestrate change

  f. What I like the least about the position:
  More unnecessary state and federal bills are being introduced that divert our attention away from the vital issues.

3. My educational achievements to date:
  a. Formal education: *BA Degree in Recreational Management*
  b. Career education (seminars, etc.): *Please note list attached*
  c. Other: _____

4. List of certifications that I have:
  Certified Association Executive (CAE)
  Certified Meeting Planner (CMP)

5. Am I interested in becoming a CEO of a not-for-profit organization?
  ___*Yes*___ (Yes/no); if yes, what is my timetable? ___*3 years*___ (years/months)

6. My estimate of expertise in and enjoyment of the following areas of work (1 being the highest):

Areas	Expertise	Enjoyment
Association management	2	1
Fiscal control	5	5
Fundraising	6	5
Staff management	3	2
Volunteer relations	2	1
Board management	7	5
Meeting planning	2	1

(continues)

Areas	Expertise	Enjoyment
Communications	1	1
Public speaking	2	1
Government affairs	1	2
Other		

7. Have I developed an advisory network? ___Yes___ (Yes/no); if yes, please describe the network:

Name	Number of Years	Describe Worth (1 being the highest)
John Nelson	10	2
Helen Smith	5	4
Henry Jones	4	3
Mary Yard	7	5
Jerry Limon	2	2

8. What is my flexibility in the position I seek?
   a. Am I willing to leave my present organization to seek new opportunities?
      Yes.
   b. Am I willing to leave my geographic area to seek new opportunities?
      Yes, but I want to stay on the East Coast.
   c. Am I willing to switch to an organization with a completely different mission?
      Yes, if I believe in the cause.

9. Do I engage myself in the community?
   a. Do I volunteer? ___Yes___ (Yes/no); if yes, please explain (1 being the highest):

Volunteer Position	Organization	Personal Worth
Vice president	Community Social	3
Coach	Son's football team	2

   b. Other:
      Play drums part time in a rock band

10. Here are the top three challenges, in my opinion, facing not-for-profits in the next ten years, and how I think they can be overcome.

Challenge	How to Overcome
a. *Perceived value*	*Make sure that not-for-profits remain vital to members*
b. *Technology*	*Make it a priority to keep up to date*
c. *Volunteers' time*	*Be flexible on what you seek*

On the other hand, Frank dislikes the fact that often a lot of unnecessary legislation is introduced. Frank feels that this takes valuable time away from work that can help strengthen his organization's mission. He realizes that the secret of success is focusing on orchestrating change over the long term while successfully performing the day-to-day aspects of a position. He also knows, however, that such a process can bog you down if you are not careful.

Question 3 of the self-assessment focuses on Frank's educational achievements. He has a solid background. Frank is a college graduate and has attended several career education courses. Frank needs to ask himself if this is enough of an educational background to satisfy a CEO search committee. For example, should he seek a graduate degree?

On the plus side, Frank has earned two major certifications, the Certified Association Executive designation, which identifies him as a seasoned association manager, and the Certified Meeting Planner certification, which identifies him as an expert in organizing major meetings.

Although this is good, Frank may want to seek other certifications to strengthen his knowledge base. For example, he may want to seek a Certified Fund Raising Executive certification to prepare him for fundraising activities because most CEOs need to raise funds to succeed.

One of the most revealing parts of Frank's self-assessment is his evaluation of how he measures up against the core areas of a not-for-profit executive's work. The areas that he feels he excels in are:

- Association management
- Staff management
- Volunteer relations
- Meeting planning
- Communications
- Public speaking
- Government affairs

The areas in which he feels he needs improvement are:

- Fiscal control
- Fundraising
- Board management

Overall, Frank has mastered a number of important skills. However, the three skills that he has identified as weaknesses are vitally important elements of the CEO function. Frank will need to find ways to master these skills. When he becomes a CEO, he may want to seek staff support in the areas of fiscal control and fundraising. As far as board management is concerned, however, Frank will need to become a master in this area himself.

Frank has an extensive list of individuals who made up his network of advisors, mentors, and colleagues. Of course, this will be a work in progress. Adding new names to this list to widen his visibility and power will be a part of his future success.

Frank seems to be flexible in his approach to seeking a CEO position. He understands that he probably will need to leave his current organization to attain a CEO position. Even though some individuals can attain the CEO position within their current organization, this is the exception. Frank understands this fact and is willing to leave to change positions.

Frank is also willing to accept a position out of town. This is a very personal question that a person must address before beginning a search. Frank is married and has three children. Everyone in his family will be affected by a move so it is important to discuss these issues with the family.

Frank is willing to be a CEO of an organization with a different mission from his current employer. His career history reveals that he has been employed by not-for-profits with varying missions in the past. Although this is acceptable, there are two important considerations to think about before you apply for a not-for-profit CEO position:

1. A CEO must believe in the mission that he or she represents.
2. Some missions are incompatible with some prospective CEOs.

CEOs who work simply to gain a regular paycheck will not serve themselves or their organizations well. A CEO must be the organization's chief advocate; a person cannot do that unless he or she is sold on the purpose of the organization.

On the other hand, compatibility is also important. Most of the CEOs who truly try but fail are often mismatched for the organizations they lead. We have all seen it happen and it is a tragedy for both the individual and the organization. Do not become a CEO of an organization unless you feel that it is a good fit.

Frank engages in the community in which he lives. This has provided him with rich volunteer experiences. He also spends a lot of time with his family and pursues recreational outlets. These are positives. CEOs need to get away from the job once in a while to lower their stress and to gain a perspective on reality outside of the corner office.

Frank seems to have a good view of the future, as evidenced by what he thought were the top three challenges facing not-for-profits in the next ten years. He also seems to know, at least in general terms, how to overcome these challenges. The purpose of this final question is to determine if Frank has the capacity to think in more global terms.

Most not-for-profit professional positions work in the present. Frank's current position is a good example. For the most part, he works to pass or defeat bills on a two-year cycle. There is an immediacy about his work—things must be done right now in order to pass a measure during this session.

CEOs must act decisively on the current agenda and, at the same time, plan for the future. Frank's CEO, for example, is concerned that Frank performs his work well to pass or defeat legislation. However, he is also thinking about the issues that will need to be addressed five to ten years from now and what needs to be done to make them possible.

Frank seems to be prepared to develop a strategic plan to ensure that his search for a CEO position is successful. In Section 4, Frank will reveal how he will set the stage to enter the search and to be successful with attaining a CEO position.

The For-Profit Executive

Over the years, I have had the pleasure of witnessing a number of for-profit professionals who have switched to positions in the not-for-profit sector. Some have been quite successful while several others have not. In my book *The Not-for-Profit CEO: How to Attain & Retain the Corner Office,* I noted that many of the aspects of conducting the day-to-day affairs of a for-profit and a not-for-profit are similar. However, there are also major differences between the two that result in a different kind of leadership style.

I can recall a man who retired from the military who had ample experience leading and administering large entities throughout his career. He was sought by both for-profit and not-for-profit employers from across the nation. Ultimately, he chose to accept a CEO position with a major national not-for-profit. From the day he entered the building until the day they told him to leave, he ran the organization as he had run his troops while he was in the service.

He ordered his staff to perform, and if they did not, he yelled at them. His leadership style was similar with his volunteer board; something that was not well received. If you tried to call him, you would be transferred to an assistant who would tell you that he was not available. He never returned phone calls, even from key volunteer leaders. He would order people to do things but never joined in to help. This man was a great leader in the military environment but was unwilling to adapt and channel his skills to a new area.

This example may seem extreme, and it probably is. After all, it is not an example of a for-profit executive entering the not-for-profit world. Yet many for-profit executives enter the not-for-profit sector believing that their skills are superior to those of people in the not-for-profit field. They often think that they can dictate under their terms how the show will be run.

There is a legitimate need to have for-profit executives enter the not-for-profit field to enhance our skill base. Likewise, there is a need for not-for-profit professionals to enter the for-profit sector to enhance that sector with the skills that they can bring to the table. Both sectors can learn a lot from how the other sector operates and how its leaders lead.

An individual who is determined to leave the for-profit sector to seek a leadership position in a not-for-profit must be prepared to approach both the search and the role of the CEO quite differently. The Self-Evaluation Tool for For-Profit Executives provides a good start in helping for-profit executives better understand how to adapt their skills to the not-for-profit environment.

Janet McGuire is a for-profit executive who is trying to determine if she wants to pursue a not-for-profit CEO position. To assist her in this quest, she has completed the self-evaluation tool (see Exhibit 3.5).

Janet has work experience in five different positions in three firms and is the vice president of sales with her current organization. Her focus has been on sales for most of her career, and, based on her record, she seems to be good at it. Janet has earned an MBA, which has helped her understand the overall aspects of business. She has also completed a number of career education courses in sales and marketing that have kept her on the cutting edge.

Janet is an active player in three professional organizations: the American Management Association (AMA), the Chamber of Commerce, and the Association of Sales Professionals. Janet finds that the AMA is a good resource for educational programs and networking opportunities. She has been active in the local Chamber of Commerce and has gained a wealth of information from the chamber's national offices, as well. Perhaps the most valuable organization for her has been a small local group, the Association of Sales Professionals, which has linked her with other sales executives who have helped her network.

Although Janet may want to retain her affiliations with these organizations, she would be wise to join associations that serve the needs of the not-for-profit community. General associations can provide her with valuable information and networking and training opportunities. One such organization is the American Society of Association Executives (ASAE). She may also want to look at some specialty organizations. For example, if one of Janet's prime roles will be fundraising, she may choose to become actively involved with the Association of Fund Raising Professionals.

To date, Janet has not needed to be certified in her field. Her MBA degree has been the key credential that has opened the right doors for her. As Janet enters the not-for-profit field, she may want to consider taking the time to obtain a Certified Association Executive (CAE) certification from ASAE. Although the CAE requires tenure, Janet can begin to work toward the certification immediately. While she does, she will gain valuable training and insight into the not-for-profit field. Janet also may want to explore several other specialty certification opportunities.

EXHIBIT 3.5   SELF-ASSESSMENT TOOL FOR FOR-PROFIT EXECUTIVES

Name: _Janet McGuire_____   Date completed: _M/D/Y_____

1. These are the for-profit positions that I have had to date:

Position	Chief Experience Gained
Sales Executive, JB Wilson and Co.	Ability to sell anything
Assistant Branch Director, Henry Forge, Inc.	Working as a team
Branch Manager, Henry Forge, Inc.	Managing people
Director of Operations, The Value Group	Fiscal control
Vice President of Sales, The Value Group	Leadership skills

2. Summary of my educational background:

Formal Education:

BA degree in Business Administration

MBA

Career Education:

Note list attached of career education courses taken in sales and management.

Other: _____

3. Professional organizations that I currently belong to:

American Management Association

Chamber of Commerce

Association of Sales Professionals (local group)

4. Certifications earned:

None

5. Have I ever volunteered? If yes, please list the experiences below:

Volunteer Position	Organization	Explain Why
Board member	Local Leukemia Society	Daughter has disease

6. Other outside interests I have:

School activities with children

7. The top five professional skills I think will make me a desirable candidate for a CEO position in a not-for-profit organization:

   a. Management skills
   b. Ability to close a deal
   c. Able to work with diverse groups
   d. Understand the fiscal aspects of an operation
   e. Able to develop a strategic plan

(continues)

EXHIBIT 3.5   SELF-ASSESSMENT TOOL FOR FOR-PROFIT EXECUTIVES *(Continued)*

8. The top three personal attributes that I feel I bring to the table:
   a. *Integrity*
   b. *Can-do attitude*
   c. *Religious faith*

9. What I feel would be the three major changes that I would have to make to successfully adapt to working in the not-for-profit community:
   a. *To understand the difference between a customer and a member*
   b. *How to motivate people who are not being paid*
   c. *The procurement of funds*

10. What I feel are the three biggest challenges that the not-for-profit sector faces in the next ten years:
    a. *Competition*
    b. *Ability to keep on the cutting edge*
    c. *How to attract professional talent*

Janet has noted on her self-assessment tool that she is currently a board member of the local Leukemia Society. Her prime motive for this is because her daughter has leukemia. Janet has helped the society to open a few doors for both volunteer leadership and funding opportunities. Her volunteer experience is one of the reasons why she is thinking about a not-for-profit CEO position at the society.

Janet takes part in activities at her children's schools. She feels that it is important for her to be involved in these activities to ensure that her children receive the best education possible. She also enjoys being part of the community and getting to know the other students' parents.

In question 7 of the self-assessment tool, Janet has listed the professional skills that she feels she possesses that will assist her in attaining a not-for-profit CEO position. Janet feels that her management skills will be a plus. It seems that she has ample experience in this area, yet will these skills be transferable, and, if so, can they be adapted to fit the not-for-profit environment?

Most of Janet's skills are quite transferable, but they will need to be adapted. The ability to work with people will be a real asset, for example, because not-for-profits often serve a cross section of people from all walks of life. Although the ability to close a deal is certainly important in the not-for-profit arena, such a term is seldom used in the not-for-profit community. The equivalent terms in this sector may include partnering, achieving a goal, or making an objective. Whatever the term that is used, it is a skill that is important to the success of a not-for-profit CEO.

Understanding and maintaining the fiscal integrity of the entity that you lead is as important in the for-profit sector as it is in the not-for-profit sector. Janet brings this strong skill to the table. The final skill she lists, the ability to develop a strategic plan, will be a major asset as well.

Many of the experiences that Janet has gained through her career can help her succeed as a not-for-profit CEO. These skills, however, will need to be refined to be used properly in the not-for-profit environment.

Professional skills are vital, but often it is the personal skills and attributes that a person brings to the table that can make the real difference. Janet believes that her strongest personal attribute is integrity. This is absolutely the number-one personal attribute that search committees look for in prospective CEOs during the interview process. The CEOs who participated in the National Study of Not-for-Profit CEOs said that integrity and trust was the chief reason why they attained and retained their positions.

Janet has also noted that she has a "can-do attitude." This personal attribute will help her a great deal in the not-for-profit community, where the key to success is often to persuade a maze of individuals and groups who may not share the same drive or mission.

It is interesting that Janet has noted her religious faith as a personal skill. The vast majority of the CEOs who participated in the study revealed that religious faith was a key contributor to their success. Janet's religious faith could be a factor in her success and the basis for her sound moral character.

Janet provided astute answers to question 9, where she was asked to list the three major changes she would have to make to adapt successfully to working in the not-for-profit community. Janet knows that, in the for-profit sector, the customer is the focal point. She understands that the not-for-profit community places the emphasis on the member. She understands that the term "member" can cover various types of individual affiliations including donors and clients. This is one of the subtle differences between the two sectors that Janet will have to fully understand in order to succeed.

Janet also realizes that different techniques need to be used to motivate volunteers. Volunteer management is both an art and an important contributor to the not-for-profit community. Persuading people to volunteer for a worthwhile cause and recognizing them for serving is one of the most rewarding aspects of work in a not-for-profit.

Procurement of funds is Janet's final major challenge. In business, you have a product or service to sell. In a not-for-profit, you are selling a mission that is designed to help others. Through that process, you encourage individuals to donate their time or funds to make that possible. It is not an easy process. It takes a great deal of skill to attract the talent and the funds required to operate a not-for-profit. Janet's sales background will help her to understand the marketing aspects of the process, but she will also need to comprehend the subtle methods used to attract the right volunteers and donors.

Janet was easily able to identify three challenges that the not-for-profit sector will face in the next ten years. This question is designed to help people understand that the primary role of the not-for-profit CEO is to prepare their organizations to successfully serve their constituents in the future.

The first area Janet identified was something quite familiar to her from her work in the for-profit sector, namely competition. In many respects, Janet may be more prepared to meet this challenge than many not-for-profit professionals, who tend to think of their organization as the only entity that can serve their mission. This is far from the reality. Most not-for-profits today are faced with competition from both for-profits and other not-for-profits.

The playing field is changing rapidly. Funding in the not-for-profit sector is becoming more challenging, and only the most innovative organizations will succeed. As a result, many not-for-profits have widened their funding base by extending their activities beyond their core mission. Thus, these organizations are entering new domains that are being successfully served by other not-for-profits. In the end, often the core area of need is not served well.

For-profits, seeing an opportunity to provide products or services in areas that not-for-profits have dominated for decades, have also entered the game. Competition is a fact of life that every not-for-profit CEO must face. The only way to succeed is to beat the competition with better products and services.

Janet identified the sector's second challenge as being the ability to keep on the cutting edge. Many not-for-profits do not take this challenge seriously and traditionally have been behind the curve in this area. Due to budget restraints, not-for-profit leaders often tend to shy away from meeting this challenge head-on. They feel they cannot afford to keep their employees on the cutting edge or provide up-to-date technology at the level of for-profits or even some other not-for-profits.

Janet's for-profit experience has taught her that keeping on the cutting edge is a sound business practice. It opens doors to new opportunities, and it also helps save overhead through better use of time and other resources.

Janet identified the sector's third challenge as the ability to attract quality professional talent. The competition factor also applies in the talent pool. Janet understands this from her experiences in the for-profit sector. Most companies focus on making sure that they have the right mix of people to stay competitive.

Upon comparing the average for-profit compensation package to the average not-for-profit package, Janet wonders how the sector can attract quality people. For-profits often provide both higher salaries and better benefits compared to similar positions in the not-for-profit community. Historically, this was due to the perception that not-for-profits lacked funds or that they did not require the same level of talent as for-profits.

Funding will always be a factor in what not-for-profits can offer employees; however, not-for-profits need the same level of talent as for-profits. Not-for-profits must function at the same quality level as any for-profit entity. The challenge for attracting quality talent is to provide the highest level of compensation possible and to make each position within a not-for-profit an exciting and rewarding experience for the employee.

Janet has the wisdom to focus on ways to find and retain quality employees who will serve her well if she assumes a not-for-profit CEO position. She will have to find ways to combine compensation, unique benefits, a unique work environment, and belief in the mission into a package that will attract and retain the employee talent that she will need.

Overall, Janet has a rich background in the for-profit sector that will be a real asset for her as she enters the not-for-profit world in her quest for a CEO position. The secret to her success will be how well she adapts her talents to fit the needs of both the not-for-profit sector and the particular organization that she will lead.

Attaining the CEO Position

No matter what your career background is or what sector you come from, the quest of attaining the corner office of a not-for-profit organization will be one of the most exciting and most challenging endeavors of your career. The companion book to this workbook, *The Not-for-Profit CEO: How to Attain & Retain the Corner Office,* provides a wealth of information that will help you to attain the corner office, particularly Chapter 2, "How Not-for-Profit CEOs Attain Their Positions," and Chapter 5, "Suggested Methods of Attaining a CEO Position."

These chapters contain detailed information that can assist you in preparing for and attaining the CEO position. To assist in the preparation, Section 4 of this text will help you begin the process.

The Current CEO

Congratulations, you have just attained a CEO position in a not-for-profit organization! It took a lot of hard work to reach this goal, including formal and career education, earning certifications, a wealth of experience in various positions, and a well-executed Career Strategic Plan to market yourself. Chapter 6 in the companion book contains detailed information on how to retain a CEO position. Many of the suggestions are from CEOs who participated in the National Study of Not-for-Profit CEOs.

One of the recommendations was that a new CEO should implement a six-month plan of action that actually begins prior to the first day of work. Exhibit 3.6 can act as a general guide to this plan. It also contains a number of specific suggestions to help you take command instantly and gather the information you need to begin to create a number of essential working documents.

EXHIBIT 3.6   A SUGGESTED PLAN FOR THE CEO'S FIRST SIX MONTHS

A new CEO can use this plan to assimilate into a leadership position while also obtaining the information needed to aggressively move the not-for-profit organization to a new level of service.

The First Day

- Meet the entire staff to immediately open dialog.
- Meet with key staff to establish relationships.
- Meet with executive office staff to establish guidelines.
- Reconfigure the new office and surroundings a bit differently from the last CEO's arrangement.
- Find out how to use core technology.
- Contact the top volunteer leader and tell her/him that you are officially on board.
- Call your old office to say that you are at the new position and if they need anything, they should not hesitate to call.

The First Week

- Meet with your key staff individually to determine functions versus reality.
- Receive an orientation on key aspects of the operation.
- Meet with each staff member one on one briefly to get a feeling for each person and to place a name with a face.
- Send a letter to all board members.
- Meet with the communications director to begin to discuss the vital role of visibility.

The First Month

- Call all board members to update them on current activities. Begin the cultivation process by visiting a few in person, if possible.
- Hold a full staff meeting and continue to hold such meetings for as long as you are there.
- Meet with key staff to discuss their working relationship with the staff.
- Make sure key staff hold weekly meetings with their staff. Drop in on the meetings once in a while.

The Second Month

- Make a trip that would feature you as the new CEO.
- Make a trip for something that is outside the mission of the organization that provides good exposure and informs your staff that you are more than just the new CEO.
- Meet in-person with more key board members or at least by conference call. Tell them that you have begun a review of the entire operations to determine its status and that you will produce The Review Document in about four months.
- Meet with entire staff to inform them about The Review Document and that you will need their help to complete it.
- Begin The Review Document by asking key staff to lead the information-gathering process.

EXHIBIT 3.6 A SUGGESTED PLAN FOR THE CEO'S FIRST SIX MONTHS *(Continued)*

- Meet with the entire board and provide them with some exciting news.
- Start walking around.

The Third Month

- Complete the first draft of The Review Document using the information gathered by the staff.
- Conduct a full staff meeting to go over the draft of The Review Document, ask their advice, and inform them how they relate to it.
- Contact key board members on a conference call to go over the draft of The Review Document and ask for their advice.
- Make changes in The Review Document based on the board's comments.
- Continue to walk around.
- Take another outside trip.
- Make a major speech on behalf of the association and obtain visibility coverage.
- Begin to selectively invite staff to lunch to ask their opinions.
- Do one major visual change in the office.

The Fourth Month

- Conduct a full staff meeting to refine The Review Document and obtain final opinions before it is presented to the executive board.
- Present The Review Document to the board's executive committee in person to seek their advice and approval.
- Refine The Review Document based on executive board comments and advice.
- Produce the final draft of The Review Document and send it around to key staff for one more look.
- Recognize a staff member for doing something right.

The Fifth Month

- Get out of your corner office more often to walk around and meet with staff.
- Get out of the overall office more with and without staff.
- Put the final touches on The Review Document and publish it.
- Begin to draft The Board Brief based on The Review Document.
- Develop an audiovisual presentation on The Board Brief.

The Sixth Month

- Present The Review Document and The Board Brief to the board.
- Find a way to make the findings of The Review Document and/or The Board Brief known to the full membership and maybe even the field your organization represents.
- Begin to refine the staff structure by promoting and moving people around.
- Begin to give hints of the need to create a strategic plan to find ways to meet the needs revealed in The Review Document and The Board Brief.

One of the important documents that the six-month plan suggests implementing is a Review Document (Exhibit 3.7), which provides the CEO with an opportunity to take charge by engaging both the staff and the volunteer leadership in an information-gathering process. Doing this will make sense at the beginning of a CEO's tenure; it will not be implemented easily if the new CEO waits too long. Remember, this is an information-gathering process, not a strategic planning process. Planning will come later.

The Review Document is designed to inform the new CEO of everything about the association as quickly as possible. As a result, he or she will be better equipped to develop an immediate plan of action as well as a long-term strategic plan for the future.

The list of areas covered by the Review Document is quite extensive; however, it is important to note that there may be more areas to review based on the uniqueness of each individual organization or situation. This document is not designed for the CEO to collect data; rather, it is a process that should involve as many staff members and volunteers as possible. This interaction makes the process easier to complete, and it also provides an avenue for getting everyone involved. Through this process, the staff and volunteers will become familiar with the new CEO's style of leadership, and they will begin to buy into the plans that may be produced from the document for current and future activities.

The Review Document has 12 major sections:

   I. Brief History

  II. Review of Fiscal Integrity

 III. Financial Resource Strength

 IV. Operations

  V. Board of Directors

 VI. Personnel Report

 VII. Members and/or Donors Relations

VIII. Government Affairs Function

 IX. Meetings, Educational Functions, and Other Programs

  X. Visibility Function

 XI. Volunteer Management

 XII. Recognition

Once these sections are completed, the CEO will have most of the information needed to determine the general health of the association.

Most new CEOs will have some basic knowledge of the elements contained in the 12 sections of the Review Document prior to assuming the position. The research process they engaged in before accepting the position should have yielded a lot of this basic information. New CEOs will have gathered information from the search packet

EXHIBIT 3.7   THE REVIEW DOCUMENT

This sample is designed to review one entity. If your association has more than one organization, simply adapt the materials to fit your use. The sample is provided to stimulate thought, but it is by no means complete. Individual circumstances may dictate the need to add additional information to your review.

An official review for the _____ (name of organization)

Conducted by _____, CEO   Date: _____

Purpose: This review is designed to take a quick snapshot of the _____

_____

(name of organization) to provide an overall evaluation of all its operations, services, and activities for the leadership of the organization. The findings of this study provide an opportunity to determine the next steps that may need to be taken to better serve the members of this organization and the field that it represents.

I. **Brief History**
- Year founded
- Mission then and now
- Number and description of organizations
- Key founding players
- An overview of five major accomplishments of the association
- Other areas

II. **Review of Fiscal Integrity**
- Paragraph on current accounting practices
- Summary of audits for the last three years
- List assets and liabilities
- Review of any reserve or endowment funds and their use for last three years
- Investment strategy and portfolio
- Other areas

III. **Financial Resource Strength**
- List sources of all funds for the last five years by major categories
- Is the organization receiving adequate funding to meet current needs?
- Level of funding needed to meet needs in the next five years
- Sources of future funding
- Other areas

IV. **Operations**
- Legal aspects of organization
- Insurance program

(continues)

EXHIBIT 3.7   THE REVIEW DOCUMENT *(Continued)*

- Support services currently being provided internally
- Professional services provided by outside sources
- Describe and list all plant assets:
  - Does the organization own its offices? Does it have a mortgage? Either way, describe the current status.
  - Do you lease space? If so, describe the lease, including length and terms.
  - Provide an inventory of the furnishings.
  - List other items, including recent major repairs or replacements.
- List all technology:
  - Currently in place
  - Needed
- List key documents and locations:
  - In-house
  - Safety deposit box
  - Other
- List major suppliers:
  - Banks that are used, and for what
  - Program supplies
  - Look for any conflicts of interest
  - Others
- Is there a procedures book? If so, is it up to date?
- Inventory process, a brief list of all inventory, including value and the location
- Other areas

V. **Board of Directors**
- List of board members, past and current
- Location of the board files, past and current
- Is there a current board prospect list? If not, develop one.
- Location of past board minutes and a copy of the minutes for the last year
- List roles of each board member:
  - Elected officers
  - Committee chairs
  - Project chairs
  - Other

VI. **Personnel Report**
- Current staff. Obtain a brief descriptive background including education and starting date
- Prime functions of each staff employee

EXHIBIT 3.7   THE REVIEW DOCUMENT *(Continued)*

- Who reports to whom?
- What kind of support is currently provided to the staff, including:
  - Training internally
  - External training
  - Other
- Staff positions not filled at this time and why
- Ratio of support staff to other staff
- Other

VII. Member and/or Donor Relations

- Review the prime method to attract participants, either memberships and/or donations.
- Number and categories of participants
- Description of the recruitment process
- The results in the last three years
- Other

VIII. Government Affairs Function

- Is there such a function? If so, describe role.
- Is there a political action committee (PAC)?
- Other

IX. Meetings, Educational Functions, and Other Programs

- List all meetings.
- Complete the meeting and program evaluation sheet for each function.
- Determine your immediate action and possible action for the future.
- Other

X. Visibility Function

- List of internal publications and materials
- List of external releases sent in the last year
- List of media placement in the last year
- Support materials for staff to use to:
  - Train
  - Make speeches
  - Other
- Support for volunteers:
  - Train
  - Make speeches
  - Other

(continues)

EXHIBIT 3.7 THE REVIEW DOCUMENT *(Continued)*

- Audiovisual materials, including radio and television applications, if any
- Web page(s) and usage
- E-mail use
- Other

XI. Volunteer Management
- Current role of volunteers
- Support program for volunteers
- Management's role
- Other

XII. Recognition—What kind of recognitions currently exist for:
- Volunteers
- Staff
- Others

---

they received, from their own research, from direct contacts with volunteer leaders and staff, and from other sources. The document is designed to verify this information, to uncover any hidden problems, and to find a treasure or two.

Gathering a brief history of the organization may seem rather basic, but you can never assume that the written history is totally accurate. This process is designed to have the research participants go back to the origins of the organization to revisit why it was formed in the first place. Has the organization's mission changed over the years? What kind of growing pains has it had? Has the organization really made a difference?

Through this process, new CEOs will be able to determine if the organization is still on the right track. They might also discover some possible gems that they can use to sell the organization's mission in the future. Perhaps they may even come across a past volunteer leader who could be a source of information or funding.

A review of the fiscal integrity of the organization is imperative. An astute CEO candidate will have made a thorough review of the organization's fiscal operations prior to accepting the position. This review is designed to look at the process in detail after you accept the position.

New CEOs will want to know if the current accounting practices meet minimum standards, including internal and external checks and balances. They will also want to verify the overall health of the organization by obtaining details on the major ways funds are procured and the current investment plans. Finally, new CEOs will want to visit the organization's accounting firm to review past audits and to ask for ways to improve fiscal integrity.

The Financial Resource Strength review is an opportunity to look into all the sources of income to determine which sources are strong and which sources are weak. Say, for example, the organization's income depends on its annual meeting to produce 35 percent of its annual income, and in the last two years the net income has increased 2 percent per year. What conclusion can be drawn? Although there may be a number of variables, on the surface, it looks like the annual meeting will need to be more profitable or other funding avenues will be needed to make up for the shortfall. This kind of information, discovered right at the beginning of a CEO's tenure, can be invaluable.

A complete review of the operations often reveals a lot about an organization. CEOs who have knowledge of this process at the beginning of their tenure will be able to function more effectively.

New CEOs will want to make sure that the legal aspects of the organization are on solid ground. A visit to the organization's legal counsel is a first logical step in this process. CEOs should review all of the organization's legal documents with the legal counsel and ask if any legal action has taken place in the last ten years. In addition, new CEOs should ask their counsel if there is anything the organization can do to improve its operations from a legal perspective.

New CEOs should not assume anything when it comes to what the organization actually owns. CEOs must understand exactly what is owned, leased, or borrowed and should know where to find anything of importance—documents, bank books, inventory lists, procedure books, and the like. This is important; CEOs must make sure that everything they think is there is really there. This review will also reveal the technology that is in place at the association. Although the office may look cutting edge, the review may turn up an antiquated computer system for example.

A complete review of the board of directors is also an important exercise. CEOs report to this group; the board has the power to retain or fire the CEO. It also holds the keys to making both the new CEO and the organization successful. It is important to have details on all current board members and an overview on all past board members, living and dead. This information will give the CEO a valuable sense of history and may even open up possible networking and funding opportunities. The review will also reveal the governance process. Of importance is who reports to whom. Even though a new CEO may be informed about the current governance process, it is always interesting to see how that process has evolved over the years.

The Personnel Report is a valuable tool for every new CEO. It provides detailed information on the current staff, their functions, how these functions relate to the overall mission, who reports to whom and why, and the types of training they have. Often staff positions are not consistent with what needs to be done or staff members have not been matched well to function. Staff refinements are not difficult to put into place early in the new CEO's tenure.

A Member and/or Donor Relations review is a must. Members and donors are the organization's chief customers, and the way the organization caters to their needs is the key to attracting and retaining them. First of all, CEOs need to know what kinds of customers the organization has. Often there are several types, including members, donors, sponsors, buyers, and even other not-for-profits. All of them are important to the success of the organization and need to be treated on an individual basis. New CEOs should make sure that the current member relations plan includes a marketing plan to attract new members and a plan to retain existing members.

The Government Affairs Function review is designed to discover how much emphasis is being placed on this important area. Most organizations fall into one of three categories:

1. They do not have a government affairs function.

2. They have a government affairs function that is, in reality, a public relations function.

3. They have a government affairs function size that is appropriate for their size and mission.

Most not-for-profits, including 501(c)3 organizations, should represent their members through a government affairs function. This function should be of a quality and a size that really serves the members. The "public relations" method does not provide proper service to an organization's members.

The Visibility Function is one of the more important areas to review. Not-for-profit organizations often do wonderful things, but if no one knows that the organization is doing them, it cannot attract members or donors. Exposure can take many forms. The key, however, is to create a consistent message that is heard in the appropriate way with regard to the organization's diverse audience.

Meeting, Educational Functions, and Other Programs review provides the CEO with the details on all of these functions. The review should specify the purpose of these functions and their value from both a member benefit and a funding standpoint. This will provide the CEO with the data needed to make the proper decisions on current activities and future refinements. It is best to have a standard evaluation process for all these activities so they can be measured equally for worth and content. Exhibit 3.8 provides a suggested format that a CEO can use as a base. The CD-ROM includes a blank copy of this sheet. I encourage you to personalize the evaluation process to fit a particular organization's needs.

The Visibility Function of any not-for-profit is vital to its success. The support materials therefore need to be appropriate and timely. The review will provide you with what is in place and what will need to be created.

The Volunteer Management review provides an opportunity to see how volunteers are procured, how they are trained, and how they may be retooled for other volunteer assignments. The key to success for most not-for-profits is the pool of quality volunteers. Volunteer management is an art and is needed more than ever due to the limited time most individuals have in today's hectic world.

EXHIBIT 3.8   MEETING AND PROGRAM EVALUATION
SHEET

Function: _____

Department: _____

Staff Assigned: _____

Volunteer Chair: _____

1. Volunteers Involved, Including Titles and Descriptions:

   Individual   Title   Description
   _____
   _____
   _____
   _____
   _____
   _____

2. History of the Meeting or Program:

   a. Date started _____

   b. Original purpose; if the purpose is different now, detail why
   _____
   _____

   c. Original volunteers and staff involved, if known
   _____
   _____
   _____
   _____

   d. Was it, and is it, considered a revenue producer?
   _____
   _____
   _____

   e. Other factors discovered
   _____
   _____
   _____

(continues)

EXHIBIT 3.8 MEETING AND PROGRAM EVALUATION
SHEET *(Continued)*

3. Description of the Function
   a. List the staff time it takes to produce the activity, counting both preparation and cleanup _____ (hours)
   b. Number of volunteers needed _____
   c. Attach a costs analysis, including staff time and all sources of income and expenses over the last five years
   d. Other

   _____

   _____

   _____

4. Evaluation Questions
   a. Does the activity fulfill an important need? _____ (Yes/no)
   b. What is the attendance record for the last five years?

      1. _____
      2. _____
      3. _____
      4. _____
      5. _____

   c. Has the event produced enough income to break even or make money?

Income	Expenses	+/−
1.		
2.		
3.		
4.		
5.		

   d. Has the event had competition from other sources? _____ (Yes/no)
      If yes, list the competition:

Competitor	How They Compete	Possible Ways to Counter

EXHIBIT 3.8   MEETING AND PROGRAM EVALUATION
SHEET *(Continued)*

e. Should the association continue to conduct this event? _____ (Yes/no)
    If so, do you recommend any refinements?

    _____

    _____

    _____

    _____

f. If not, would this event be missed if it was dropped? _____ (Yes/no). If yes:

    1. Could this program be combined or merged into another program or activity?
        _____ (Yes/no)

    2. Can the association afford to drop the program? _____ (Yes/no)

    3. If the program was dropped, what other activities could take its place?
        Please list:

        _____

        _____

        _____

        _____

    4. If the event is marginal, could it be phased out over time? _____ (Yes/no)

        _____

        _____

        _____

        _____

        _____

        _____

    5. Other Comments

        _____

        _____

        _____

        _____

        _____

        _____

(continues)

EXHIBIT 3.8 MEETING AND PROGRAM EVALUATION
SHEET *(Continued)*

6. Future Status of the Activity
   (Outline recommendations based on your evaluation.)

_____

_____

_____

_____

_____

_____

_____

_____

_____

_____

Director of the Department   Date

_____

Chief Executive Officer   Date

It is important to be aware of the organization's current volunteer culture and its future needs. Exhibit 3.9 provides a starting point for the new CEO to begin to evaluate the existing volunteer plan and to determine the activities and programs that can be expanded if additional volunteers were in place. The CD-ROM that accompanies this workbook includes a blank copy of this sheet.

For more detailed information on how to create a comprehensive volunteer management plan, refer to my book *The Universal Benefits of Volunteering*, published by John Wiley & Sons.

Recognition is important because recognition is a crucial role that needs to be played within a not-for-profit organization. Volunteers need to be recognized for the work they do for the organization. Besides being the right thing to do, recognition encourages further involvement and attracts others to volunteer.

Staff members also need to be recognized. Many not-for-profit employees have made financial sacrifices to work in the field, and most are dedicated to the missions that they serve. Staff members who are recognized for their work tend to do more to ensure the continued success of the organization, often in functions unrelated to their job description. A comprehensive recognition program should involve everyone, including donors and others who support the cause.

EXHIBIT 3.9   THE VOLUNTEER EVALUATION FORM

Department: _____

Description of the Current Volunteer Program:

_____
_____
_____
_____
_____
_____
_____
_____

Describe the Volunteer Management Plan:

_____
_____
_____
_____
_____
_____
_____
_____

- Number of staff supporting the effort _____
- Management process _____
  _____
- Recognition program _____
  _____
- Evaluation program _____
  _____
- Other _____
  _____
  _____
  _____
  _____

(continues)

EXHIBIT 3.9   THE VOLUNTEER EVALUATION FORM *(Continued)*

List of Current Programs and Activities in Which Volunteers Are Used

Activity	Current Volunteers	Volunteers Needed

Activities and Programs that Could Be in Place if Volunteers Could Be Secured

Activity	Number of Volunteers Required

Signature of Department Head   Date

Chief Executive Officer   Date

A comprehensive Review Document with attachments is a very large package, condensed to fit into a large binder, and the CEO and other staff members may wish to have it handy for reference for a period of time.

The Review Document should be presented officially to the board to show members the depth of review that was performed. For practical reasons, the document should be condensed into a "board brief," which is simply a workable version of the Review Document that contains a summary of the research findings. Suggestions for creating a board brief can be found in Chapter 6 of the companion book, *The Not-for-Profit CEO: How to Attain & Retain the Corner Office*.

THE TIME TO MOVE ON

One of the most difficult decisions a CEO has to make is determining the right time to seek a new position. The reasons for doing so tend to vary from person to person, but the decision is normally based on one or more of these factors:

- A feeling of being bored and a desire to move on
- Wanting to fulfill a larger role
- A hint that you may have stayed too long at the dance

Often successful CEOs, particularly those who consider themselves change agents, begin to get bored after they have overcome the initial challenges that they faced when they first became the CEO. They now find themselves performing the day-to-day routines that are required to keep the not-for-profit afloat. The organization has been turned around, and they find it easy to keep it heading in the right direction. To keep the job interesting, they often add a new element or two into the mix, but the excitement that they once felt is no longer there.

Not all CEOs feel this way, however. Some of the participants in the National Study of Not-for-Profit CEOs stated that they were content to stay with one organization for their entire career, making it better and better each year. These leaders have found their golden opportunity, and all is well. However, for those who get the itch to move on, they and their organizations may be better served if they seek a new adventure.

Successful CEOs tend to have egos, and these egos tend to push them to do bigger and better things. Astute CEOs, however, try not to get carried away with such feelings. They take time to measure each new opportunity to make sure that they do not make the wrong move. Wanting to fulfill a larger role is a normal reaction of successful people; if the opportunity arises, it should be investigated in a businesslike manner.

A hint that you may have stayed too long is another feeling that CEOs get from time to time. Not-for-profit CEOs are fired frequently, and often the CEO is the last person to recognize the telltale signs. CEOs should always have their antennae up for the warning signals. Most of the clues will come from the volunteer leadership or the staff. The primary sign is often the "pushing away process," where a CEO may find that he is suddenly less in the loop with volunteers or staff. If this is your situation, it may be too late to change course, and an exit plan may be in order.

In many cases, CEOs often have a successful record at the not-for-profit. Hidden agendas and politics are often the cause of their downfalls. It is unfortunate, yet it is one of the things that a CEO has to deal with.

The companion book to this workbook devotes two chapters to retaining the CEO position — Chapters 3 and 6 — and one chapter to attaining the CEO position — Chapter 7.

Ralph Moore is a successful CEO at Youth Center, Inc. Exhibit 2.6 provides a brief overview of his background. His profile clearly shows that Ralph has ample credentials, including a strong academic background, career education experiences, work experience, networking, and outside interests.

Ralph understands that he will need to develop a Career Strategic Plan to begin the process of conducting a search to attain a new CEO position with greater responsibilities. Ralph's plan can be found in Section 4: The Career Strategic Planner. Ralph knew that he should do a self-evaluation to document the key aspects of his past experience, to begin to analyze what steps he might need to take in a strategic plan and to begin to think about the type of organization that he might wish to lead. To assist him in the process, he completed the Self-Assessment Tool (Exhibit 3.10).

Ralph's self-assessment provides a good place for him to start his search. As he looks into what he might need for his strategic plan, Ralph may need to add other comments or categories to the self-assessment.

Ralph began by evaluating his current and past positions. He focused on what he accomplished for the organizations as well as what he personally gained from each experience. Search committees will look for career achievement in resumes, but they are also interested in what the candidates retained from those experiences. After all, they seek someone who can reproduce these achievements in their organization.

Ralph has listed only the chief experience he gained from each activity. He may want to document these and other experiences in story form. Such stories provide vivid examples that highlight a candidate's skills during an interview process.

One of Ralph's strong points is his educational background. His solid academic background may be the key to attaining certain CEO positions, particularly positions within educational associations. Ralph also has an extensive career education background. The attached list shows the courses he has taken throughout his career.

Clearly, Ralph understands that keeping on the cutting edge requires professionals to continue to seek educational opportunities. Ralph has also taken courses to fulfill the volunteer roles he has held. These courses have helped him to perform these roles better, and his volunteer experiences have helped him to more fully understand the volunteer act from the perspective of the individual performing the function.

EXHIBIT 3.10	SELF-ASSESSMENT TOOL FOR CEOS WHO SEEK HIGHER LEADERSHIP OPPORTUNITIES

Name: _Ralph Moore_   Date completed: _M/D/Y_

1. My past and current positions:

Position/Organization	Chief Experience Gained
Assistant District Executive/Boys Club of America	Volunteer management
District Executive/Boys Clubs of America	Staff management
Fundraising Director/Community Services, Inc.	Fundraising
Vice President-Government Affairs/Youth Centers	Administration
President/Youth Centers	Leadership

2. Educational background:

Formal Education:

BA degree in Business Administration

MS degree in History

Ph.D. degree in History

Career Education:

(Please note attached career education courses listed)

Other:

Courses taken as a volunteer

3. Current professional organizations that I belong to:

Organizations	Chief Reason Why
Association of Fund Raising Professionals	Maintain FR skills — leadership opportunities
American Society of Association Executives	Networking with CEOs — leadership opportunities

4. Certifications that I have earned:

Certifications	Benefit
Certified Fund Raising Executive (CFRE)	Identifies me as seasoned fundraiser; recertification helps me keep on the cutting edge.
Certified Association Executive (CAE)	Identifies me as a seasoned association professional; recertification helps me to keep on the cutting edge

5. Do I have volunteer experience? _Yes_ (Yes/no); if yes, please explain:

Position/Organization	Experience
Volunteer counselor/City Works Program	Helping disadvantaged youth

(continues)

EXHIBIT 3.10   SELF-ASSESSMENT TOOL FOR CEOS
WHO SEEK HIGHER LEADERSHIP
OPPORTUNITIES *(Continued)*

6. My other outside interests include:

Interest	Why
Outdoor sports — hunting, fishing, and boating	*Great stress reliever and it helps me to better understand our role in nature*

7. Here are five professional skills that I feel make me a desirable candidate for a higher CEO position:
   a. *I excel in both the fiscal control and fund procurement.*
   b. *Due to my academic background, I tend to analyze everything.*
   c. *I enjoy working and supporting volunteers.*
   d. *I believe in the team approach and work with staff.*
   e. *I continually look for better and more efficient ways to fulfill mission.*

8. These are the top three attributes that I bring to the table:
   a. *I have a can-do attitude.*
   b. *I feel that my work is a calling.*
   c. *I feel I have integrity and can be trusted.*

9. These are the skills that I feel I will need to brush up on or attain prior to conducting my search:

   While I am a seasoned not-for-profit professional, brushing up on methods to operate a large and perhaps multilocation operation will help me to attain and retain a larger CEO opportunity.

10. Here are the top three challenges that I feel not-for-profits will face in the next ten years:
   a. *Funding*
   b. *Competition*
   c. *Volunteer support*

Ralph has also been active with two professional organizations, the Association of Fund Raising Professionals and the American Society of Association Executives. Both organizations have provided a number of personal benefits to enrich his professional life. Like most professional associations, education is the primary reason for participating, but Ralph also listed other benefits, including leadership opportunities, networking, and maintaining skill levels.

Ralph has taken advantage of his participation by becoming a volunteer leader of both organizations at the local level. He has used these opportunities to enlarge his group of personal advisors, which will become an asset to him as he begins his search.

Ralph has also been able to maintain his skill level by taking advantage of career education opportunities and one-on-one discussions with key players.

Due to Ralph's zeal for both experience and continued education, he has attained and continues to renew two significant certifications, the Certified Association Executive (CAE) certification and the Certified Fund Raising Executive (CFRE) certification. Both certifications have helped him to be more successful in his career and to be recognized by both staff and key volunteer leaders as a seasoned professional.

There are, of course, other certifications that may be of help, depending on the nature of the not-for-profit in question. A lack of certifications may not prevent a person from attaining a CEO position, but certifications do provide additional experience opportunities. More important, a certification may be the competitive edge that opens the right door at the right time.

Question 5 asks if you have ever volunteered. This may seem irrelevant, but it really is not. Professional leaders, particularly CEOs, who continue to volunteer throughout their career have a much better knowledge of the entire volunteer process. Volunteering can often open doors to networking or CEO opportunities. Ralph has volunteered with another organization to help disadvantaged youths.

Ralph has several outside interests, including hunting, fishing, and boating. These activities help him relieve stress and enjoy the outdoors. These outside activities are healthy for Ralph's well-being, and they help him to relate to volunteers, funding sources, and the general public. Search committees are often as interested in a CEO candidate's outside interests as they are in traditional credentials. Volunteers seek well-rounded leaders.

Ralph has listed the professional skills that he has mastered that will make him a desirable CEO candidate. Among his skills are some of the most sought-after experiences that search committees desire. Fiscal control and fund procurement is generally the number-one concern of not-for-profit boards. They seek someone who can provide expert advice and who can produce results. They want a candidate who will share the burden of fiscal responsibility equally.

They want a candidate who can balance the books by keeping expenses down and revenue up. They also want a CEO who knows how to find the money. Although not-for-profits vary in sources of revenue, astute CEOs know how to maximize current revenue sources as well as finding new ones.

Ralph's academic background may provide him with an edge. While he was writing his dissertation, Ralph found that the methods used to conduct his research could very easily be applied to the planning process in not-for-profit organizations. In practice, he found that volunteers really like this approach because the resulting plan is based on a research model rather than just the opinions of the leader.

Ralph has also indicated that he enjoys working with and supporting volunteers. Search committees are hungry for someone with experience in volunteer management, but they have a voracious appetite for professionals like Ralph who "get it." Ralph volunteers himself, so he understands what it takes to support a volunteer in the field.

Boards want a strong staff leader, one who can inspire people and get things done through others. They want a CEO who can handle all of the staff issues and use staff talents to fulfill the mission of the association. Ralph has indicated that he is on a continual search for better and more efficient ways to fulfill the mission of his organization. Most not-for-profits need this skill today. With budget restraints and a continually changing playing field, the CEO must be an active player in finding ways to make things happen.

Ralph listed his best personal attributes on his self-assessment tool. Among Ralph's attributes are a can-do attitude and the fact that he feels his job is a calling and that he prides himself on his integrity and trust. A can-do attitude is a must for any not-for-profit CEO position. Successful not-for-profit leaders need to be self-motivated and need to find ways to get the job done.

Like Ralph, most CEOs who participated in the study felt their work was a calling. Truly successful CEOs do not think of their jobs as merely a way of making a living; rather, they think of their jobs as a way to make a contribution to society. These CEOs are proud and pleased to have the opportunity to serve.

Selecting a new CEO who possesses integrity and trust is a major priority of search committees. If Ralph can convey these qualities, he will have a good chance of being a finalist in any search.

Question 9 asked Ralph if there were any areas in which he needs to improve. This can be a difficult question to answer, but it is important to set your ego aside and to be honest. Ralph feels that he needs to become more familiar with what it would take to operate a large, multilocation operation. This is a good idea because the type of organization that Ralph seeks to lead will have to be administered differently than his current association. In fact, the ability to lead larger organizations will probably be one of the questions he will encounter from search committees.

Ralph finally let us know what he thought were the top three challenges that not-for-profits will face in the next ten years. To answer this question, the CEO candidate must be a student of history and a predictor of the future. Astute CEOs are adept at reading signs and trends; they must always have an eye towards the future. Ralph concluded that the three major challenges facing not-for-profits in the next ten years include:

1. **Finding new funding sources.** Ralph is correct—many traditional funding sources will change or even vanish. Innovative CEOs who are good at discovering new sources of funding will be highly sought after.

2. **Competition.** Many not-for-profit leaders are unaware of this trend. Astute CEOs embrace this trend as an opportunity to show their constituency that their association is the best in the field.

3. **Volunteer support.** Securing such support will become even more challenging due to the time restraints of current and potential volunteers and competition from other organizations. Ralph knows that individuals always will be attracted to volunteer for organizations that are well organized, focused on their mission, and have good brand recognition.

Ralph feels that the self-assessment tool has helped him to better understand himself and the kind of CEO position he might want to seek. He understands that he must analyze the data and make a determination of whether he wants to seek another CEO position.

SUMMARY

Getting things done is the name of the game when it comes to preparing yourself for a lifelong career. Regardless of your current status—high school student, college student, professional in the field, a for-profit executive, or a current not-for-profit CEO—the desire to occupy the corner office can be strong. Not everyone will have this privilege, but it will never happen if you do not try. By approaching the process in an organized and methodical way, your chances will only increase.

There is nothing magical about the process. As the National Study of Not-for-Profit CEOs indicates, the participating CEOs have worked hard for their position. They have higher than average academic credentials, and they believe in lifelong education. They have a wealth of past experience, and they have a can-do attitude. Yet each of them has unique traits that set them apart from others. Most important, however, they all have a spark or a drive in them that pushes them to succeed.

CEO hopefuls need to prepare for their ultimate dream. One of the best ways to do this is to conduct an honest self-assessment—often and at various stages in your career. The self-assessment will act as guide to developing a Career Strategic Plan. The strategic plan will need to be updated regularly, but that is the exciting part. The plan is adaptable and is with you at every stage of your career.

The Career Strategic Planner

Some men see things as they are and say, why? I dream things that never were and say, why not?

—George Bernard Shaw

INTRODUCTION

The search for the corner office begins the moment that someone determines that he or she wants to become a CEO of a not-for-profit. This section is designed to assist prospective CEO candidates in transforming their hopes and desires into a plan of action. In some cases, this plan will take years to complete, in other cases, it may take only weeks or months. In either case, the corner office awaits those who understand how to both attain and, more important, retain the position.

THE PLANNING PROCESS

To begin the strategic planning process, you will need to have completed a personal analysis and the self-assessment tool. It is impossible to form a strategic plan unless you are fully aware of your strengths and weaknesses. Prior sections of this workbook have covered the personal analysis and the Self-Assessment Tool. If you have completed these documents, you are now ready to use this information to create your Career Strategic Plan.

One of the important parts about this process is keeping the content fresh and flexible. To do this, you will need to set aside times to review the plan and to refine your approach. How often you have to do this depends on a number of variables including age, career goals, and environment.

It is normal for things to change. Your professional direction may change from time to time, as may your personal goals and family situation. The important thing is to keep a watchful eye on your career and to make sure that you make the right decisions as opportunities come your way. If you are in the game, you will be surprised at the number of opportunities that arise.

It is important to keep your Career Strategic Plan up to date so you can maximize these opportunities. At the very least, you should update the plan once a year. You must also have in place a process by which you can update the plan easily if a change or opportunity comes your way. The plan needs to be flexible enough to react to both positive and negative circumstances. An up-to-date Career Strategic Plan will provide you with a structure to refer to when opportunities come your way.

The key to the planning process is flexibility. Everything is in constant change. CEO hopefuls need to understand this and be able to take advantage of these changes. Change is often feared, but, ironically, it is the time when opportunity is at its greatest. Successful CEOs welcome change and find ways to take advantage of it as much as possible. Change is an interesting phenomenon—it closes some doors but, at the same time, opens many others. The art is finding the best doors open to you.

Career development is like a chess game. Many times new players do not see an opportunity until it is too late. Successful players, however, anticipate the moves and are able to react to changes very quickly. Aspiring CEOs need to discover the right methods and resources to keep up on the trends within their profession. Ways to keep up include reading industry publications, researching on the Internet, and actually practicing being a change agent yourself.

The desire to achieve success comes from inside. It is often the result of wanting to make a difference for you as well as for others. True success, however, is not a selfish thing; it is the ability to make a universal difference for as many people as possible. Sadly, some people do not want to succeed, and often they place roadblocks in their way to ensure that their wish comes true. These same individuals may not want you to succeed either, and they may place obstacles in your way, too. This is part of the negative effects that future leaders must deal with in their quest for the corner office. Do not ever get discouraged; just find ways to get around the negativity.

TIME, ENERGY, AND A SENSE OF HUMOR

The CEOs who participated in the National Study of Not-for-Profit CEOs were clear that the road to the corner office is not necessarily that complicated; you simply have to earn it. Obviously, there are exceptions to this rule: people who are seemingly in the right place at the right time and get the position well before the norm. However, it is important that CEO hopefuls focus on their own individual reality and never give up until the goal is achieved.

The study revealed that past experience is the key to attaining a CEO position, so putting in your time is quite important. Yet the type of experiences that you have along the way can make a difference. A CEO's chief role is to lead. The only way to know how to lead is to have some experience doing it. Therefore, the Career Strategic Plan should focus on how to gain leadership experiences.

Energy is another trait of successful leaders. Energy is part of the winning attitude that successful people project to everyone around them. It is contagious, and it improves everyone's level of performance. It is important to be a part of activities or organizations that you feel enthusiastic about so that you can project this kind of energy.

A sense of humor is a very important tool to have. Humor can help relieve tension, open doors, turn a negative situation into a positive situation, and help to build a team effort. Humor can make an organization sizzle. A proper blend of humor can help to resolve any issue—even serious ones—and makes work more enjoyable for everyone. In addition, humor is one of the best ways to attract and retain both volunteers and staff.

THE PERSONALIZED CAREER STRATEGIC PLAN

A Career Strategic Plan is a personal thing. Yours will not match those of your friends, coworkers, or supervisors. It is designed to keep you on track toward a goal, in this case the CEO position. It can be used for any position, however. This is important to note because your Career Strategic Plan can help you achieve a number of positions on your way to the corner office.

Successful people often see themselves as the center of a wheel when it comes to their careers. This does not mean that they have a me-only attitude, but rather that they recognize the truth that no one is more interested in their career than they are.

Think of yourself as a precious stone. A diamond needs to be cut and polished to have any value—but it also needs to be marketed properly to the right customers to command the best price. Obviously, you will need to have the right mix of education and experience to be qualified to be a CEO. All of that preparation is worthless, however, unless you market yourself properly.

The Career Strategic Plan outlined in this section is a general base to follow. It is purposely designed to be flexible so that you can adapt it to fit the specifics of your situation. Career planning is a lifetime exercise. To be successful, you will be planning until you retire; some people even keep a plan going in retirement to stay active.

Each of the example career planners has completed an individual research phase by completing the Self-Evaluation Form and/or the Self-Assessment Tool. In each case, these tools have helped them to determine that they wish to embark on the journey to the corner office. Now they will complete a Career Strategic Plan.

High School Student: Theresa Rodriguez's Career Strategic Plan

It may seem too early for a high school student to develop a career strategy and, in some ways, it is. However, for individuals who are very serious about their goals at this age, it will help them stay ahead of the pack. Completing a Career Strategic Plan is never a waste of time, even if career goals change.

Theresa Rodriguez has completed the Self-Assessment for High School Students (Exhibit 3.2), which has helped her focus on a number of issues she needs to address. She realizes that she will need to make some important decisions about her future in the next year. While she is still very much in the investigative stage, she knows that all of her career choices will require higher education.

Her immediate challenge, therefore, is to shop for good schools and to be accepted into college. She will also need to figure out how she is going to pay for college. To assist in this process, Theresa has completed the Career Strategic Planner for High School Students (see Exhibit 4.1). A blank copy of the planner is available on the CD-ROM that accompanies this workbook.

In her plan, Theresa has listed her five career choices by rank. She does not want to eliminate any of her choices, but she wants to focus on the top three: Athletic Coach, Activities Director, and Journalist. This was a wise move. This gives her time to investigate these choices and perhaps replace one or more with another choice.

Theresa wants to seek some outside educational opportunities to help her determine if she would like one of her top three career choices. She also figures that it will help her school grades. She is going to start by trying to find educational programs focusing on English and writing.

Theresa is also going to investigate how she can get practical experience in coaching and activities work. She has seen others perform these tasks but is unaware of the requirements for these positions.

Her most immediate challenge, however, is to get accepted into a college and to figure out how to pay for it. She knows that her GPA is average, but she figures that she can still get accepted at a number of state schools. She had not taken the SAT yet, but she is taking a prep course and will be prepared to take it in the spring.

Theresa wants to earn a degree that could be a base for her career. She feels that a major in business, sociology, or journalism would provide a sound base for some of the careers she is interested in. Her plan is to minor in subjects that are more specific to current or future career choices.

Theresa wants to make sure that she picks the right college from both an academic and a financial standpoint. She has asked her high school advisor to point her in the right direction, but she knows that she will need to be in charge of the process.

Her parents are supportive and will help as much as possible in the process. Theresa will supplement this help with online research and other data that she needs to make a sound decision. She will ask her mentors to suggest the best schools and the best coursework to pursue. Finally, Theresa and her parents will visit the leading schools.

Theresa's biggest challenge will be paying for college. She is willing to work to help, but it will not be enough. She knows that her parents will help her as much as they

EXHIBIT 4.1   THE CAREER STRATEGIC PLANNER FOR HIGH SCHOOL STUDENTS

Name: *Theresa Rodriguez*   Date updated: *M/D/Y*

Grade: *High School Junior*

Date expect to graduate: *M/D/Y*

1. Based on my Self-Assessment, these are the career areas that I wish to pursue:
   a. *Athletic coach*
   b. *Activities director*
   c. *Journalist*
   d. *History teacher*
   e. *Lawyer*

2. Here are the additional classroom experiences that I seek to take while in high school:
   a. *Additional work in English*
   b. *More experience in writing skills*

3. I wish to explore these outside educational opportunities:
   I need to determine what opportunities I should seek.

4. Here are the additional outside activities that I feel would be beneficial for me to explore:
   a. *Find a way to experience what a coaching position would be like.*
   b. *Explore the role of an activities director in a not-for-profit.*

5. Based on current thought, do I need to plan to attend college? ___*Yes*___ (Yes/no); if yes, list the following:
   a. Do I have the academic standing to secure a college slot?
      - Are my grades high enough? ___*Maybe*___ (Yes/no)
      - If not, are there alternative ways?
        Not sure.
      - Have I taken the SAT? ___*No*___ (Yes/no)
      - If yes, is the score high enough to secure a college slot?
        _____ (Yes/no)
      - If no, are there alternative ways?
        Currently studying and will take the SAT soon.
   b. What do I feel would be the best major(s) to study in college?
      - *Business administration*
      - *Journalism*
      - *Sociology*

(continues)

   c. How will I investigate and select the best college for me to attend?
- *Through my high school counselor*
- *Advisors, including parents*
- *Online*
- *In-person visits*

   d. How will I finance my education?
- *Part-time job*
- *Help from parents*
- *Loans*
- *Grants*

6. Based on the information contained in the first five questions, here is my first draft of my Career Strategic Plan.
   a. *Gather information on my five career choices.*
   b. *Focus on the top three career choices to determine if they should remain in contention.*
   c. *Seek outside educational opportunities to become more proficient in English and writing.*
   d. *Investigate how I can get practical experience coaching and as an activities director.*
   e. *Prepare to take the SAT.*
   f. *Investigate potential colleges.*
   g. *Determine the best major and minor to initially take.*
   h. *Work with my advisors including my high school counselor, mentors, and parents for advice and support.*
   i. *Find ways to pay for college.*

7. I will share my plan with key advisors including my parents, high school counselor, and others to ask their advice to help me refine the plan and help me to begin the process.

Remember to:
   a. Check off your completed goals.
   b. Add new components that you discover are needed.
   c. Do a complete review of your plan at least twice a year.

---

can, but she will still need to get scholarships or loans. Since she is an average student, loans will probably be the most realistic avenue.

After compiling her Career Strategic Planner, Theresa decided that she must address and consider these areas:

- Gathering information on the top five career choices

- Focusing on the top three career choices to determine if they should remain in contention
- Seeking outside educational opportunities to become more proficient in English and writing
- Investigating how to get practical experience in coaching or as an activities director
- Preparing to take the SAT
- Investigating potential colleges
- Determining the best major and minor for college
- Working with advisors including her high school counselor, mentors, and parents for advice and support
- Finding ways to pay for college

Once Theresa completed her first draft of the plan, she asked her mentors and advisors to go over it and make suggestions and refinements.

- Her advisors agreed it was wise to continue the information-gathering process for the top five career choices.
- They also thought that Theresa was wise to focus on the top three career choices. They pointed out that she should remain open to the possibility of focusing on a career choice outside the top three and, possibly, one that did not even make the list. They reminded her that this is all about the journey.
- Her advisors were impressed with the idea of seeking educational opportunities outside of school to determine if a journalism career would suit her. They suggested seeking assistance in helping her increase her grade point average with an eye toward securing some type of scholarship.
- They agreed that it was wise to acquire actual experience as a coach or an activities director. Every job has its good points; it also has negative areas that are often overwhelming. Having firsthand experience is the only way to tell if you like a field for sure.
- Her advisors urged her to prepare for the SAT. They told her that this should be her number-one priority. A higher score will mean being accepted to more colleges and, maybe, the possibility of a scholarship.
- They were impressed that she is shopping for colleges so early. They suggested that she should expand her focus to both public and private schools. They also suggested expanding her geographical search to a 500-mile radius from home.
- Her advisors were impressed that she has already given consideration to possible majors and minors. They suggested making sure that the college that she selects has more than one of her top choices in case she changes her mind.
- Her advisors were honored to be asked to help, and they encouraged Theresa to come back anytime.

- They also advised her that it is never too early to find ways to pay for college. They suggested asking prospective schools about financial aid and scholarships as well as enlisting the aid of her high school counselor.

Theresa's Plan

Career Phase 1: Education and Research	Due Dates
1. Develop a plan to collect information on my five top career choices.	3 months
2. Focus on the top three choices and test the waters.	12 months
3. Seek educational opportunities outside school for English, writing, and course improvement.	6 months
4. Seek opportunities to experience what careers would be like in coaching and as an activities director.	12 months
5. Continue to prepare for the SAT.	6 months
6. Begin to search for colleges and universities.	12 months
7. Determine to best major and minor to take in college.	12 months
8. Keep in touch with advisors to seek their wisdom and support.	ongoing
9. Find ways to underwrite the cost of college.	15 months

Theresa Rodriguez has developed a brief but inclusive plan that will help her achieve success in the first phase of her career. In many ways, these are the most important steps that we make as we begin to ascend the career ladder.

Theresa's Success Story

Theresa Rodriguez's Career Strategic Plan was well reasoned. She followed the spirit of the plan and was wise enough to make it flexible so she could adapt it as necessary. Her planning and hard work paid off.

Theresa kept the files on all five career choices, and they became quite full. However, she continued to focus on her top three choices. Coaching was the first to go. It was replaced by counseling.

Theresa took classes in English at a local community center and was happy to discover that the textbook was the same one she used in her high school English class. The community center offered courses in writing that Theresa took and found fascinating. She also took a few courses in mathematics and biology, which helped her raise her GPA.

Theresa found some opportunities to work with a few coaches and an activities director. She learned that she was not interested in becoming a coach but that the activities director position seemed promising. The executive director of the athletic center spent some time with her and made her aware of the kinds of careers that are available in the not-for-profit sector.

THE PERSONALIZED CAREER STRATEGIC PLAN

Theresa focused on her SAT preparation, and the effort really paid off. She scored high, and with her recently increased GPA, she was in fair shape to be accepted by a number of colleges.

Theresa began her search for colleges that would be a good fit. She visited four schools near her home. She ended up applying to two state universities with good reputations and reasonable tuition. In addition, she also applied to a private college about 100 miles from her home based on the recommendation of her high school counselor.

Theresa approached an executive director of a local not-for-profit for career advice, and he ended up becoming a mentor to her. He told her to check out American Humanics, Inc., an organization that supports colleges and universities offering degrees in not-for-profit administration. American Humanics directed her to two schools near her home. One happened to be one of the state schools that she had already applied for.

This school had the majors and minors that Theresa was looking for, so she was delighted when she was accepted. Theresa was also able to underwrite the cost of college through a combination of two part-time jobs, parental support, a small grant, and financial aid.

She decided to major in not-for-profit administration with a minor in journalism. Theresa immediately updated her Career Strategic Plan upon entering college, and she adapted it throughout her college years. She continued to be an active volunteer during college, and she found rewarding work each summer for different not-for-profits to gain more practical experience. In addition, she wrote for the school newspaper and became the editor.

Theresa is near the end of her junior year in college. She is expanding her Career Strategic Plan to prepare for her first search for a professional position. Theresa hopes that she can secure a position in a not-for-profit organization.

Theresa continued to maintain her group of advisors who supported her during her college search. She also was fortunate to gain additional advisors during her college years through school, work, and volunteering contacts. These advisors will be crucial in her search for her first professional position.

College Student: Lewis Johnston's Career Strategic Planner

Theresa Rodriguez had some idea of what she might like to do for a career. Although it was vague, at least she had a place to start. Many students have no idea what they want to do. Every person is different—some want to pursue a career that gives something back to the community, some want the highest-paying job possible, and others would rather party and not think about it.

Ideally, you should aspire to a career that has meaning for you and some worth to the community. The important thing is to choose a career that you really enjoy doing. You will spend most of your adult life working, so why not invest a little time to determine what you would like to do and putting a plan in place to accomplish it? If you really enjoy what you are doing, success and money usually will follow.

Most careers require at least an undergraduate degree. Employers require this due to the knowledge base, maturity factor, and perseverance that a college degree requires. Therefore, it is important to earn the degree, but it is also important to make the most of the experience. This requires taking the college coursework as well as taking advantage of internships, leadership opportunities, outside work, and extracurricular activities.

Lewis Johnston's background summary can be found in Exhibit 1.3. He is a typical college student who is working part time to help pay his way through school. An average student, he is involved in college activities and has a number of positive outside interests. He has completed the Self-Assessment Tool (Exhibit 3.3) to assist him in beginning to develop his Career Strategic Plan. Lewis's Career Strategic Plan can be found in Exhibit 4.2. A blank copy of the Career Strategic Planner for College Students can be found on the CD-ROM that accompanies this workbook.

Lewis began to outline his strategic plan by:

1. Listing three possible careers
2. Determining if he wants to seek additional classroom experience in six areas
3. Exploring outside educational experiences
4. Exploring outside work experiences to test the waters
5. Considering graduate school prior to pursuing a career
6. Beginning to investigate possible employers to seek a position after college
7. Developing a Career Strategic Plan based on his research
8. Sharing the plan with his advisors

Lewis asked his advisors to review his plan and to suggest refinements or improvements. Lewis's group of advisors includes his parents, a teacher from high school, his baseball coach, the assistant director of the community service club, a local business executive who is on the board of a community service club, and a police officer in charge of the PAL program where he volunteers.

Lewis's plan is to continue to investigate three career choices—for-profit management, sales/marketing, and not-for-profit management. His advisors feel that his career choices fit well with his major in business administration and his minor in accounting and with Lewis's aspirations.

His advisors agree with his list of additional college courses that he wants to take to round out his academic background. His advisors were impressed with the fact that the accounting and management courses reinforce his business major and that the creative writing, planning, and Spanish courses will help him to expand his horizons. His advisors suggested some coursework in sociology to prepare him for the realities of the community.

EXHIBIT 4.2   THE CAREER STRATEGIC PLANNER FOR
COLLEGE STUDENTS

Name: _Lewis Johnston_____   Date Completed: _M/D/Y_____

Current Grade Point Average: ___B___   Date I Expect to Graduate: _M/D/Y___

1. Based on my Self-Assessment, these are the career areas I wish to pursue:
   For-profit management
   Sales/marketing
   Not-for-profit management

2. Here are the additional courses that I wish to take while in college:
   Additional accounting courses
   Management
   Sociology
   Creative writing
   Additional Spanish courses
   Planning

3. Should I explore any outside educational opportunities?
   Yes, courses at other institutions that would help me round out my educational experience.

4. Here is my plan to pursue other outside activities that would be beneficial for me to explore:
   - _Find either part-time work or an internship with a for-profit._
   - _Find part-time work, an internship, or volunteer opportunities at a not-for-profit._

5. Should I consider a graduate degree before I pursue my career?
   I feel that I should investigate the need and possibilities.

6. If I intend to seek career employment after undergraduate school:
   a. Do I have any prospective employers in mind? _Yes_ (Yes/no).
      If so, have I conducted any research on them?
      Yes, but I need to do more.
   b. What type of position do I seek?
      - _I want to enjoy my work._
      - _Make a difference in some way._
      - _I want a career and the ability to advance._
      - _It must have the status of a professional position._
   c. What compensation would I like to receive?
      Enough to provide for my family
   d. What preparation do I feel will be needed to secure employment?
      Not sure, I need to investigate.

(continues)

EXHIBIT 4.2   THE CAREER STRATEGIC PLANNER FOR
COLLEGE STUDENTS *(Continued)*

7. Based on the information contained in the first six questions, here is my first draft of my Career Strategic Plan:
   a. *List three possible careers.*
   b. *Determine if I want to seek additional classroom experiences in six areas.*
   c. *Explore outside educational experience.*
   d. *Explore outside work experiences to test the waters.*
   e. *Consider graduate school prior to pursuing a career.*
   f. *Begin to investigate possible employers to seek a position after college.*
   g. *Develop a full Career Strategic Plan based on the research gained.*
   h. *Share the plan with my advisors.*

8. I will share the plan with my key advisors, including my parents, college counselors, and others, to ask their advice to help me refine the plan and to begin the process.
   I need to find ways to build my network of advisors and to make it a habit to ask them for help and support.

Remember to:
   a. Check off completed work.
   b. Add new components that you discover are needed.
   c. Do a complete review of your plan at least twice a year.

His advisors also suggested that he might want to take a few courses at other colleges in the area. One alerted him that a small college in town had a major in not-for-profit administration. Coursework from this institution would be very valuable if he decides to pursue a not-for-profit career. Other schools were mentioned for marketing and sales courses.

His advisors urged him to pursue outside activities that would give him an opportunity to discover if his current choices for careers were appropriate. One of his advisors even offered Lewis a job at his office.

His advisors discussed the possibility of pursuing a graduate degree. They suggested that an advanced degree would be an asset in some of the career areas that Lewis is pursuing. At the same time, they know that Lewis is working his way through school and that it may not be practical for him to pursue a graduate degree immediately. One or two suggested that a future employer might encourage or even pay for graduate school.

His advisors encouraged Lewis to begin to look for employers in the next year or so. They cautioned him that it would be premature to seek actual jobs, but it would provide him with some ideas of what may be available in a few years. They strongly suggested that he measure these employers and some general job descriptions against his criteria for the ideal job. This way, he can begin to rank his career choices and eliminate some from the list.

Lewis's Plan

Career Phase 1: Education and Research	Due Dates
1. Develop a plan to find out as much as possible about the three career choices that I have made.	12 months
2. Develop a plan to make sure that I am able to take the additional college courses and complete them before I graduate.	12 months
3. Explore outside educational opportunities at other schools that can round out my academic package.	12 months
4. Determine when and if I should pursue a graduate degree.	12 months

Career Phase 2: The Pre-Search Process	Due Dates
1. Begin to gather information on prospective employers.	3 months
2. Select two employers per career choice and contact them for information on possible careers.	6 months
3. If possible, determine the top one or two career areas.	12 months

Career Phase 3: The Search Process	Due Dates
1. Develop a resume and cover letters.	18 months
2. Use college counseling and other services to identify positions.	6 months
3. Alert my network of advisors that my search process has begun.	12 months
4. Alert the employers that I investigated that I am now seeking employment.	20 months
5. Secure a professional position.	24 months

Lewis's three-phase plan is designed to focus on the areas that he needs to secure a professional position in a not-for-profit organization, and he has set rough due dates for each. This is a plan in motion, and it will require constant refinement and updating. Even if Lewis chooses another career, the process itself will be a good planning experience for him.

Lewis's Success Story

Lewis Johnston developed a two-year plan to accomplish a number of objectives. His plan included completing undergraduate school with a maximum learning experience, gaining outside experiences, selecting a career area that best fit him, and conducting a successful search for his first professional position.

Lewis began to concentrate his efforts on the three career areas that he wished to investigate. He gathered information from a number of sources, including his college library, professors at school, various online sites, advisors, and places that he worked and volunteered. He began to see that all three of his career interests were related in some way, and he wondered if there might be a career opportunity that would be a hybrid of these choices.

Lewis developed a plan to ensure that he was able to take the coursework he wanted. It was good that he planned this coursework well in advance since two of the courses he needed were only taught every other year. Lewis really enjoyed the courses in his major, and he could see how his elective coursework in planning and creative writing supported his major. He felt that his studies in sociology provided a good base, as well.

Lewis investigated other colleges in his area for additional coursework that was not available at his own university. The college that offered a degree in not-for-profit administration offered a number of courses that interested him. Lewis was not sure if he wanted to devote his career to this field, but he did decide to take some courses in governance and leadership anyway. He really enjoyed these classes and was able to receive full credit for them at his own university.

Lewis also pursued the internship from his advisor, who worked in a local business and brought Lewis in to help on a marketing campaign. Lewis enjoyed this work and was able to write some copy for the campaign. Later he was given the opportunity to work as a volunteer for another advisor, who is the assistant director of the community service center. She made it a point to give Lewis a full hands-on experience — Lewis learned everything about how not-for-profits function, from fiscal controls to raising funds.

After careful consideration, Lewis made the decision to hold off on pursuing a graduate degree. He felt ready to start his career and wanted to begin to pay back his loans. However, he is planning to pursue the graduate degree program in the future.

After working hard and doing his homework, Lewis was ready to move into phase two of his Career Strategic Plan. He gathered information about prospective employees both locally and nationally. His advisors were a big help here. Each of them gave him great ideas and even opened a few doors.

At this point, Lewis discovered another career choice that embraced all three of his top career choices. Although the fit was not perfect, it was a very good solution in his quest to have it all. Lewis found a company that managed a number of not-for-profits. One of his advisors had mentioned the firm and arranged to have Lewis meet the owner. Lewis focused his career choice on either a for-profit or a not-for-profit management position. He found that his desire to be in marketing/sales could be satisfied through either avenue.

As Lewis began phase three of his Career Strategic Plan, he had successfully completed his education, research, and pre-search process phases. It was easy for him to develop a resume — he had the academic credentials, a great mix of courses, practical experience in a number of areas, internships, and writing skills. Lewis produced an exceptional one-page resume and cover letter. He also had a dynamite follow-up letter ready.

Lewis used the resources at his college to conduct his job search. He also asked his advisors to help and contacted the employers he investigated during his research phase. He relied on cold calling as well as contacts and networking. As a result, Lewis received calls from four prospective employers including a local accounting firm, a national not-for-profit with a local office in the area, the community service club where he volunteered, and the firm that manages the not-for-profit organizations.

Lewis turned down the accounting firm's offer as he felt that he was not cut out to be an accountant. He interviewed with the three remaining employers. The community service club had an opening, but it was not a management position. The national not-for-profit organization with local offices offered Lewis a management position out of town. Finally, the not-for-profit management firm offered him an opportunity to become an account representative where he would manage four not-for-profits.

Lewis had a hard decision to make. Ultimately, he chose the not-for-profit management firm because he felt that would satisfy all of his career goals at the same time.

Lewis has been quite successful at the management firm. In fact, the owner of the firm has promoted him a twice over the last eight years. Lewis currently manages three other account executives. Lewis has continued to seek career training. He has also been active in the American Society of Association Executives and its local allied group. He has earned his Certified Association Executive (CAE) certification and just recently his master's degree in not-for-profit administration.

Lately Lewis has been updating his Career Strategic Planner to determine the feasibility of conducting a search for a CEO position in a not-for-profit organization. Although he enjoys his current role, he is eager for another challenge and feels that he can give back a little more to the community if he pursues a job in the corner office.

Professional in the Field: Frank Fulton's Career Strategic Planner

Frank Fulton has done his homework. He has completed the Not-for-Profit CEO Position Self-Evaluation Form for Professionals in the Field (Exhibit 2.3) and the Self-Assessment Tool for Professionals in the Field (Exhibit 3.4). This has provided him with a wealth of information to begin the process of developing his Career Strategic Planner.

Once he began the process of crafting his Career Strategic Planner, he realized that this was not going to be a one-time exercise but, rather, a continual process that he can use for the rest of his career to ensure that he maintains the momentum he desires. Frank wishes that he had started this process much earlier in his career. Exhibit 4.3 shows Frank's Career Strategic Planner. A blank copy of the Career Strategic Plan for Professionals in the Field can be found on the CD-ROM that accompanies this workbook.

Frank took a careful look at his Self-Assessment, his professional background, and his personal desires and decided that he would be open to any well-governed association with a mission he was comfortable with. This left a large number of organizations open to Frank: perhaps too many.

EXHIBIT 4.3   THE CAREER STRATEGIC PLANNER FOR
PROFESSIONALS IN THE FIELD

Name: *Frank Fulton*   Date completed: *M/D/Y*

Current position title: *Vice President*
Employer: *New Jersey Society of Home Growers*
Location: *Stillwater, New Jersey*
Number of years at current employer: *4*
Number of years at current position: *4*

1. Based on my Self-Assessment:
   a. What mission and/or kind of not-for-profit do I seek in my next not-for-profit?
      Associations with missions that I can be comfortable with and that are well governed.
   b. What is the time frame for the search? *3 years*
   c. Other unique areas: *I want to make sure that my leadership style fits the prospective organizations.*

2. Do I feel that my academic and career education background is satisfactory?
   __*No*__ (Yes/no); if no, what additional education do I need?
   a. *Would like to complete a master's degree program*
   b. *Need to acquire skills in fundraising*
   c. *Would like to have additional experience working with boards of directors*

3. Do I feel that my outside activities are sufficient at this time?
   __*Yes*__ (Yes/no); if no, what additional activities do I feel are needed?

   _____

   _____

   _____

   _____

4. Based on the information contained in the previous questions, from the preliminary overview and my Self-Assessment Tool, here is my first draft of my Career Strategic Plan:
   a. *Seek to attain a master's degree in 18 months.*
   b. *Take coursework in board relations and fundraising.*
   c. *Gain practical experience in working with boards and fundraising.*
   d. *Find ways to make myself more visible.*
   e. *Work my network and use it to create new opportunities.*
   f. *Create appropriate versions of my resume.*
   g. *Develop various letters of introduction.*
   h. *Begin to obtain hard copy and online sources for job openings.*

   i. *Create opportunities to write and speak.*

   j. *Look for opportunities to speak to key volunteers of targeted associations.*

5. Upon sharing my plan with my key mentors and associates to ask them their advice to refine or enhance my plan and to begin the process, here is my second draft of my Career Strategic Plan.

6. Here is my formal search process:

   a. *Develop talking points for inquiries.*

   b. *Test intro letters and resumes.*

   c. *Contact search firms to inquire if they have positions that may fit my search requirements.*

7. Here is how I will prepare for the interview process:

   a. *Research the organization online and by other means.*

   b. *Ask for as much information as possible from the organization.*

   c. *Prepare for the meeting — rehearse.*

   d. *Follow up with key people.*

Remember to:

   a. Check off your completed work.

   b. Add new components that you discover are needed.

   c. Do a complete review of the plan at least twice a year.

Frank has worked for a variety of associations, but he will need to focus his search. He is determined not to rush; he is willing take up to three years to search for the right CEO position. This may seem like a long time, but his search could include a testing process and some self-improvement.

Frank is being careful to make sure that his leadership style will fit well with prospective organizations. He had seen many professionals go from organizations where they have been very successful to other not-for-profits where they have failed. He is convinced these failures had to do with having the wrong leadership style for the organization.

Frank has earned an undergraduate degree and has kept on the cutting edge through career education and by earning two certifications. Still, he feels that he needs to acquire additional training and credentialing. He would like to earn a master's degree to be more competitive and would like to find ways to gain fundraising skills and experience with working with boards. This is why Frank has developed a three-year search plan.

Frank's concerns regarding education and experience are valid. In reality, he could conduct a search and go to graduate school at the same time. If his search produced an opportunity before he earned his degree, the fact that he is seeking the degree would impress the search committee.

Frank's concerns about gaining fundraising skills and board experience are different, however. These two skills are the keys to success for most CEOs, and he is wise to pursue ways to gain more knowledge and practical experience in these areas. Several institutions offer career education in these areas. Frank could use the information from these classes in a practical application in his current association or through volunteer experiences.

Frank feels like his plate is pretty full and that he has enough outside activities at this time to keep him up to speed. Frank is wise to admit this. Often executives try to do too much and end up doing little or nothing well. Successful people tend to focus on top priorities and delegate other functions, even though they really enjoy doing those activities.

Frank has completed his Career Strategic Planner (Exhibit 4.3). A blank form for your use can be found on the CD-ROM that accompanies this workbook.

Frank Fulton's Plan

Frank has set the goals for his Career Strategic Plan:

1. Earn a master's degree in 18 months.
2. Take coursework in board relations and fundraising.
3. Gain practical experience in working with boards and fundraising.
4. Find ways to make myself more visible.
5. Add to my network and use it to create new opportunities.
6. Create appropriate versions of my resume.
7. Develop various letters of introduction.
8. Find sources for job openings.
9. Create opportunities to write and to speak.
10. Look for opportunities to speak to key volunteers of targeted associations.

Upon completing the first draft of his plan, Frank met with his mentors and advisors to ask their opinions on refining and enhancing the plan. His advisors had these suggestions:

1. Seeking a master's degree is a great idea. Here are your options:
   a. It may be best to complete the degree prior to starting your search. Then you can declare it on your resume.
   b. You can begin your degree and your search at the same time. Just let prospective search committees know. It may not be as effective as having a degree, but it shows that you intend to complete it.

    c. Let the search committees know that you intend to seek a degree in the next three years. Be sure to let them know that you are flexible on this time-line—it could impact your chances of landing the position depending on how the search committee envisions the new CEO spending his or her time.

2. Taking the coursework on board relations and fundraising is a great idea. Use this information and training to dazzle search committees.

3. Having additional experience with regard to boards and fundraising is good, too. Let search committees know that you intend to learn as much as possible before, during, and after the search process.

4. Developing a plan to make yourself more visible during the search process is a great idea. Do not stop there—continue finding ways to do this for the rest of your career.

5. Figure out who in your existing network can help you and determine whom you need to add to your network. Go out and proactively seek the people who can help you.

6. Develop a base resume that is quickly adaptable for specific situations. Come up with three or four different versions of the resume for the more common situations you encounter so you are ready to move on a position when it opens up.

7. Do the same thing with the introduction letter—create a base letter that is quickly adaptable and several versions for more common situations.

8. Seek out key sources of job openings. This includes your network, headhunters, cold calls to organizations that you have researched, industry publications, and so on.

9. Writing and speaking are great ways to increase visibility and experience.

10. Once you have targeted an association, find someone in your network who can open a door for you. This is much better than walking in cold.

Although Frank's mentors and key advisors did not add much to his list, they did provide a few sound suggestions, and, more importantly, they verified most of what he thought would be the key points of his Career Strategic Plan. Of course, it is still up to Frank to make the final decision on how or if to proceed.

Frank Fulton's Plan

Frank wants to make sure that he is fully prepared for his first CEO position. Based on the research he conducted, he developed a three-year plan with four phases.

Career Phase 1: Education and Experience	Due Dates
1. Earn a master's degree.	18 months
2. Take courses in board relations.	12 months

Career Phase 1: Education and Experience *(Continued)*	Due Dates
3. Find ways to acquire practical experience working with boards.	24 months
4. Take courses in fundraising.	12 months
5. Find a way to acquire practical experience in fundraising.	24 months

Career Phase 2: Visibility, Research, and Documentation	Due Dates
1. Become more visible in the local area.	12 months
2. Become more visible at the national level.	24 months
3. Add appropriate people to my network.	18 months
4. Work my network to seek opportunities.	24 months
5. Find ways to write for the field.	12 months
6. Orchestrate speaking opportunities.	12 months

Career Phase 3: The Pre-Search Process	Due Dates
1. Determine the kind of not-for-profit that I wish to seek.	12 months
2. Begin to tap into the search process to seek what is available.	18 months
3. Test basic resume and create other versions.	24 months
4. Test introduction letters.	24 months
5. Contact search firms to alert them to my search.	24 months

Career Phase 4: The Search Process	Due Dates
1. Alert my network that the search process has begun.	25 months
2. Make sure that other key players know that I am in the market.	25 months
3. Send search documents to prospective opportunities.	25 months
4. Secure a CEO position.	36 months

Frank's four-phase plan is designed to accomplish certain objectives by due dates. The time frames were set on sort of a building block effect. This plan may play out exactly as it has been set, but chances are it will not. There will be delays or even an unexpected job opportunity that will force Frank to refine it. The important thing is that the plan remains flexible.

Prepare for the Interview Process

If Frank sticks to his plan, he will begin to receive inquiries from search committees or headhunters. When that happens, Frank will be prepared to respond. Responding includes the ability to:

- Quickly research the organization in question
- Quickly refer to a prepared outline in case someone calls unexpectedly inquiring about your interest in a job and wanting to know a few details about your background

- Quickly produce additional materials that may be requested unexpectedly, including writing samples, lists of published articles, lists of speaking engagements, and so on
- Refer to a basic outline and procedure to prepare for an interview
- Send thank you letters and other supporting information within 24 hours of the interview

Of course, many of these materials and responses will need to be tailored for each specific organization. However, having access to basic outlines, procedures, and documents will save a lot of valuable time and will allow you to focus on making your responses much more dynamic and exciting.

Frank Fulton's Success Story

Frank Fulton spent more time than most in preparing his formal search, but it paid off. Frank decided to enter graduate school, and he earned his master's degree in business management in 18 months. He found one of the new degree programs that combines classroom time with online learning, so he was able to fit it into his busy schedule.

In addition, Frank found a great course on how to deal with not-for-profit boards. It gave him a much better understanding of the role that CEOs play. Frank asked his current CEO if he could attend board meetings to get a better idea of how the board really functions. The CEO let him attend, and when he discovered that Frank was looking to become a CEO, he became one of his new mentors.

Frank asked a local not-for-profit CEO who is a friend how to learn the art of fundraising. The CEO gave him information on local and national education programs conducted by the Association of Fund Raising Professionals. In addition, he asked Frank to volunteer for his organization and provided him with a wealth of practical experience in fundraising.

Frank found ways to become more visible through his professional and personal activities. He asked to take over a controversial issue that his association was working on that had received a lot of media coverage. In addition, he also was given an award from a community social service organization for his volunteer contributions. The award ceremony was covered by a local TV station.

Frank offered to speak on not-for-profit issues at the local affiliate of the American Society of Association Executives (ASAE). His talk was so well received that he was encouraged to apply to conduct a seminar at ASAE's next national meeting. His application was accepted, and his seminar was a hit. Frank met a lot of new people through his public speaking and even secured two new advisors for his network.

Frank immediately began to cultivate these new additions. As a result of his new visibility, several local and national writing opportunities came his way. Each of these opportunities provided him with more visibility and helped Frank to gain more confidence.

Frank began to think about the kind of not-for-profit that he would like to run as a CEO. He decided that he would like to find a national organization that had links to what he liked to do as a volunteer within the social service community. He began to search for these organizations and found that most were headquartered in either Chicago or Washington, D.C.

Altogether, he found 37 organizations that seemed to have the right fit. He researched all of them and developed files on each that he could refer to. He began to develop a draft resume and introduction letters that might be used in a search.

He even tested the waters—during the course of his research, three of these organizations were conducting a search for a CEO. He applied for one position but was not offered the job. So he contacted the search firm and asked why he was not chosen. He discovered that they wanted someone who was a practitioner in the field. He began to think that perhaps he was looking at the search from the wrong perspective.

Testing the waters some more, he contacted a couple other search firms to ask if they had any positions that would fit his profile. Again, he found that many of the associations wanted a practitioner from the respective field rather than a professional association executive. One headhunter suggested that Frank may want to alter his search toward a trade or a professional society.

Frank gave this some thought and refined his search plan to include trade and professional societies—but he still wanted to find a position that related to his dream. By the end of the second year, Frank was ready. He had done his homework, he knew what he wanted, and he had the materials and network to formally launch his search. He began to seek positions aggressively.

In three months, two opportunities had come his way. He turned down the first offer. After conducting his research on the organization, he found a couple of problems during the interview process. One was the fiscal health of the organization, the other was the governance structure. He also found that the past two CEOs were fired after less than two years in the position. Frank notified the search committee that he was not interested.

One of his mentors called him up about a week later and informed him that the Community Social Service Professional Association was about to begin a search for a new CEO. The current CEO was retiring, and the organization was looking for someone who had a diverse background and a lot of government affairs experience. His mentor, a good friend of the retiring CEO, said that he could probably arrange an interview for Frank.

Frank accepted his mentor's invitation and the interview was arranged. The search committee was so impressed that they offered Frank the position the day after the interview. Frank negotiated a three-year contract. He was so successful in his first two years that he was given a five-year extension. Frank has been the CEO of the association for six years now and is starting to think that it may be time to look for even greater leadership opportunities.

For-Profit Executive: Janet McGuire's Career Strategic Planner

Janet McGuire has had a successful for-profit career, and it never even occurred to her to seek a not-for-profit position. However, she was approached by the local Leukemia Society to consider becoming a candidate for the CEO position as a result of her work as a volunteer. The offer intrigued her, but it caught her by surprise and she felt that she needed to take the time to fully evaluate the opportunity from a career perspective.

Janet completed the Self-Evaluator for For-Profit Executives (Exhibit 2.5) to determine if such a change in her career would be wise or desirable. In addition, she completed the Self-Assessment Tool for For-Profit Executives (Exhibit 3.5) to determine if she had enough transferable skills and to find out if her perceptions of the not-for-profit field were accurate.

As a result of these evaluations, Janet concluded that the opportunity was worth investigating further and decided to complete a Career Strategic Plan (see Exhibit 4.4). A blank copy of the Career Strategic Plan for For-Profit Executives can be found on the CD-ROM that accompanies this workbook.

Janet is a seasoned for-profit executive, and, frankly, she is not altogether sold on this opportunity. She likes the idea of being a CEO and helping an organization that she really believes in to succeed, but she is not sure if this is the right move from a career standpoint. That is why she was not totally enthusiastic in her rating when she asked if she wanted to pursue this position. She feels that additional investigation is in order before she can fully commit.

Janet realizes that the search committee's time frame is very short. The current CEO is going to retire, but he will not leave until they find a qualified person to take his place. The current CEO has been with the society for over 20 years, and he has done a remarkable job with fundraising. Janet realizes that one of the big benefits of assuming this position is that the current CEO is willing to act as an advisor to the next CEO after he leaves. She is also aware that he has recommended her for this position.

Janet feels confident that her academic and business background will be a real asset for her in this position. At the same time, she also realizes that she will need to get up to speed on the operations and culture of a not-for-profit. She knows that she will need to take extensive training as well as rely on others for while, but she is confident that she can be successful.

Janet completed her Career Strategic Plan based on her current knowledge of the CEO position at the Leukemia Society and her for-profit background.

EXHIBIT 4.4   THE CAREER STRATEGIC PLANNER FOR
FOR-PROFIT EXECUTIVES

Name: *Janet McGuire*   Date completed: *M/D/Y*

Current Position Title: *Vice President of Sales*

Employer: *The Value Group*

Location: *Spokane, Washington*

Number of years at current employer: *12 years*

Number of years at current position: *7 years*

1. On a scale of 1 to 10 with 1 being the highest, I rate my determination to secure a professional leadership position in a not-for-profit organization as a # __*7*__ .

   Please explain the answer:

   I was not seeking a not-for-profit position, I was approached. After looking into the possibilities, I am taking a serious look but I am not committed yet.

2. The type of not-for-profit organizations that I seek to lead and my proposed time frame.

   Please explain:

   I have been asked to head the local Leukemia Society.

   The search process, as far as I know, is about six to nine months.

3. I feel that my academic and career education background is sufficient.

   __*No*__ (Yes/no); if no, these are the additional educational programs that I need:

   While I have earned an MBA degree and have kept up with my career education, I feel that if I accept this position, I will need to develop a plan to take courses in not-for-profit administration.

4. Here are the additional activities to assist me in my transition:

   a. *I have been active in a number of external organizations that have helped me keep visible and network in my current position. It may be wise to continue to be active with some of them.*

   b. *I will need to become active with the appropriate organizations that would help me to work more effectively in the not-for-profit arena and in particular for the Leukemia Society.*

5. Based on the information gathered from my research, here is my first draft of my Career Strategic Plan:

   a. *Determine if I wish to be a candidate for the CEO position at the Leukemia Society.*

   b. *If I accept the invitation, determine the search process and how I will react to it.*

   c. *Develop a learning plan to get up to speed.*

   d. *Determine the networking plan for such a position.*

   e. *Alert my advisors to my decision and ask for help.*

EXHIBIT 4.4 THE CAREER STRATEGIC PLANNER FOR FOR-PROFIT EXECUTIVES *(Continued)*

   f. *Develop my search process.*

   g. *Prepare for the interview process.*

6. Upon sharing my plan with my key advisors to ask them their advice to refine or enhance my plan and to begin the process, here is my second draft of my Career Strategic Plan.

7. Here is my suggested formal search process:

   a. *Develop talking points.*

   b. *Create the intro letter and resume.*

   c. *Cultivate volunteer leaders.*

8. Here is my suggested interview process:

   a. *Research the organization online and by other means.*

   b. *Ask for as much information as possible from the organization.*

   c. *Prepare for the meeting—rehearse.*

   d. *Follow up with key people.*

Remember to:

   a. Check off your completed work.

   b. Add new components that you discovered are needed.

   c. Do a complete review of the plan at least twice a year.

Career Phase 1: Education and Experience	**Due Dates**
1. Determine if I wish to be a candidate for the CEO position at the Leukemia Society.	2 weeks
2. If I accept the invitation, determine how I will handle the search process and how I will react to it.	2 weeks
3. Develop a learning plan to get up to speed.	4 weeks

Career Phase 2: Visibility, Research, and Documentation	**Due Dates**
1. Determine my networking plan for this position.	8 weeks
2. Alert my advisors to my decision and ask for help.	8 weeks

Career Phase 3: The Pre-Search Process	**Due Date**
1. Develop my search process based on a not-for-profit model.	10 weeks

Career Phase 4: The Search Process	**Due Dates**
1. Prepare for the interview process.	12 weeks
2. Secure the CEO position.	15 months

Janet has wisely asked her current advisors for help. They have been one of the keys to her success for most of her career. Janet started developing her network of advisors early in her career. They consist of two college professors, her first boss, a handful of top business executives including a couple of CEOs with whom she has worked over the years. Janet asked them to look over her Career Strategic Plan and to provide her with their thoughts and ideas.

They all strongly suggested that Janet needs to decide quickly if she wants to pursue the position. Her advisors did not try to encourage or discourage her. Janet decided to measure her current position against the CEO position to determine the positives and negatives based on her long-range career goals.

Her advisors agreed and recommended that Janet meet with the current CEO to get an idea of the current health of the organization and a general idea of the compensation package. Janet has had access to many of the organization's important documents in her role as a volunteer, but she requested copies so she can review them in more detail.

The advisors have suggested that Janet find out more about the search process as soon as possible so she can determine how she fits into it.

- Will she need to prepare anything other than a resume?
- Will she receive preferential treatment since she was asked to be a candidate?

Janet's advisors agreed that she has a wonderful business background that could help the Leukemia Society but that she also needs to learn quickly how the not-for-profit community functions and how the society fits within that community.

The advisors did not have to tell Janet about networking; after all, they are part of her network. But they did encourage her to seek a whole new network within the not-for-profit community to help her to succeed in this demanding arena.

The advisors told Janet to develop the search process as if she were seeking a position at an unknown association. They suggested that others may have been asked to be candidates, as well, and they told Janet to ask the current CEO about this. Either way, the advisors told her to go for the position if that is her decision.

The advisors encouraged Janet to also prepare for the interview process. They advised her to go into the interview with two or three goals in mind:

1. Sell yourself to the search committee.
2. Make them want you as their CEO.
3. Provide them with a vision on how you will lead their organization.

Janet was pleased with her advisors' suggestions, which reinforced the plan that she developed and gave her a few ideas that she can use to dazzle the search committee.

Janet McGuire's Success Story

Janet had an unexpected opportunity to become the CEO of a not-for-profit organization, but she had to decide quickly. The most challenging part of the process came at the beginning—Janet had to determine if she actually wanted the position. Her advisors wisely suggested that she compare her current position with the proposed offer. Janet took their advice and obtained the information she needed to make a true comparison. Here is what she found:

Comparison	Current VP Position	Proposed CEO Position
Salary	$110,000	$75,000
Benefits (estimated worth)	20,000	12,000
Vacation	3 weeks	4 weeks
Incentives	$10,000 to $15,000	$7,500 to $15,000
Days off	12 days	19 days
Health benefits	Full	Full
Personal days	4 days	20 days
Commute	90 minutes	10 minutes
Out-of-town travel	60 days a year	10 days a year
Career/promotions	Good	Good

Janet had mixed feelings about the position after she had made the comparison. Clearly, her current job provides better compensation, but the new position provides more free time—something that she had been wanting for a long time.

Her decision was a lot easier to make after she spoke with her children. They were really excited about the extra time she would have at home as a result of a shorter commute and more vacation time. Janet had no illusions about the position; she knew it would take more than 40 hours per week to perform. She had seen firsthand how long the current CEO worked, but, at the end of the day, she would be near her home and she would be able to be with her children, particularly the one with leukemia. Janet decided to go for the job.

She contacted the current CEO to tell him that she was interested. He told her that she would be considered one of the final candidates and that they hoped to begin interviewing in three months. He felt that they would have no more than four final candidates by that point.

Janet went to work to gain as much information on the Leukemia Society as possible. She met with the current CEO a number of times to ask his advice. She also began to develop a plan that she could implement immediately if she secured the CEO position.

Janet also began to expand her network. She met with several not-for-profit CEOs in the area to ask questions and to get advice on what the not-for-profit community was all about. She also asked these CEOs what search committees really wanted to know. She was pleasantly surprised to hear that search committees sought what she was strongest in: management skills, marketing ability, and personal qualities such as integrity and trust.

She discovered that she would need to gain additional skills, including fundraising, board relations, and working with volunteers. Janet knew, however, that her solid business sense and personal experience would help her gain these skills quickly.

Janet developed her pre-search process by condensing all the information and experiences she encountered into a marketing plan to sell her candidacy. She began to meet with as many Leukemia Society volunteers as she could. This was easy due to her role as a volunteer. As a result of this effort, everyone on the search committee got to know Janet a little bit better.

Janet and two other candidates were invited to meet with the search committee. However, it really was no contest. Janet was well known by then, and her business and volunteer success made a winning combination. She was offered the position the next day and started two months later.

Janet has been with the Leukemia Society for nearly 12 years now. She has brought a sound business sense to the organization and has significantly increased funding and program activities. This past September, Janet's youngest child entered college, and her oldest daughter will graduate from college next year.

Janet wonders if the timing is right to begin a search for a new CEO position. She has heard from one of her advisors that a CEO position may be opening at a national health association headquartered in Washington, D.C. Her advisor told her that he knew the search committee chairman and might be able to arrange a meeting. Janet is thinking about going for it.

CEOs Who Seek Higher Leadership Opportunities: Ralph Moore's Career Strategic Planner

As a seasoned not-for-profit CEO, Ralph Moore has a pretty good idea of what needs to be done if he wants to seek a higher leadership position. His biggest challenge is deciding if he should seek the opportunity or not.

To determine if it is wise to do it, he evaluated his situation. He completed the Self-Evaluator Form to begin the process. The results can be found in Exhibit 2.7. Ralph also used the Self-Assessment Tool for CEOs Who Seek Higher Leadership Opportunities (Exhibit 3.10) to analyze his background to determine what he can provide to another not-for-profit. The process also provided him an opportunity to see what kind of organization he would seek.

Ralph knew that he would have to conduct this search a little bit differently from the search he used for his current CEO position. It had been nearly seven years since that search, and the level of his new search would be much higher. In order to begin the process, he completed the Career Strategic Plan (see Exhibit 4.5). A blank copy of the document can be found on the CD-ROM that accompanies this workbook.

Ralph's Career Strategic Plan included these steps:

Career Phase 1: Education and Experience	Due Dates
1. Seek wisdom from my advisors.	1 month
2. Determine if I really want to seek another CEO position.	2 months
3. Complete the profile of what I seek in my next position.	3 months
4. Determine the kind of training I need and complete it.	6 months
5. Create a plan to gain practical experience.	6 months

Career Phase 2: Visibility, Research, and Documentation	Due Date
1. Alert my network that I am searching for a new position.	2 months

Career Phase 3: The Pre-Search Process	Due Date
1. Develop my formal search process.	7 months

Career Phase 4: The Search Process	Due Dates
1. Prepare for the interview process.	7 months
2. Launch the marketing phase of the plan.	8 months
3. Secure a new CEO position.	12 months

Ralph then shared his plan and his aspirations with his advisors. Although he is a seasoned career not-for-profit executive and CEO, he still maintains a network of advisors that goes back to his college days. Every one of them knows Ralph well. They know what he is capable of as well as what he is not so good at. His advisors are experts in many fields; this fact has helped Ralph to better understand the many roles that a CEO must play. Ralph knew that his advisors would be honest, and that is just what he needed.

Ralph's advisors cautioned him to be very careful about making a quick move. They praised him for his current work and for his overall success. They told him that, if he assumed a new CEO position, there would be a good chance that it may not be a good fit for a number of reasons.

They reminded him that his age may factor into his decision for the first time. He could not afford to fail at his age due to the loss of income, retirement implications, and the problem of finding another job. They were not discouraging him to seek another CEO position, but they wanted him to think about the possible consequences of his actions. They also wanted him to think about the kinds of safeguards that he should insist on, including a well-executed contract.

His advisors thought that his goal of creating a detailed profile of each association that he sought to cultivate was a great idea. After all, he was satisfied with his current position and should not seek any position that did not meet his goals.

EXHIBIT 4.5   THE CAREER STRATEGIC PLANNER FOR CEOS WHO SEEK HIGHER LEADERSHIP OPPORTUNITIES

Name: *Ralph Moore*   Date Completed: *M/D/Y*

Current Position Title: *President and Chief Executive Officer*

Employer: *Youth Center, Inc.*

Location: *Atlanta, Georgia*

Number of years at current employer: *12 years*

Number of years at current position: *7 years*

1. On a scale of 1 to 10 with 1 being the highest, I rate my determination to secure a new professional leadership position at a not-for-profit organization as a # *7* .

    Please explain the answer:

    I am not sure if I want to test the waters. I have not made up my mind yet to conduct a search for a new CEO position but down deep I feel I am ready for a move.

2. The type of not-for-profit organization I will seek to lead, and my proposed time frame. Please explain:

    I have developed a list of what I would seek in an association if I determine to conduct a search:

    - *I seek a national association that is or has the capability to make a significant difference in the lives of youths.*
    - *I would like to change the type of organization that I may seek but I wish to stay within the youth-serving field.*
    - *The organization must have a sound governance policy in place.*
    - *Financial stability is an important factor.*
    - *Most important, the organization's mission has to be something that I would be comfortable leading.*

    The time frame is not as important as finding the right organization, but for planning purposes I have set a goal to secure a new position within 24 months.

3. Do I feel that my academic and career education background is sufficient?

    No (Yes/no); if no, these are the additional educational programs that I need:

    Even though I have attained a doctorate, have kept myself up-to-date through career education, and have earned and kept my certifications current, I still feel that I need additional training for the position I seek. The position will require a much higher degree of planning, delegation, and networking to be successful.

4. Here are the additional activities that will assist in my possible transition:
   - *I should seek to perform new activities that I may need to do in a new position.*
   - *I should gain some practical experience dealing with larger organizations.*
   - *I should increase my networking to discover position opportunities.*

5. Based on the information gathered from my research, here is the first draft of my Career Strategic Plan.
   a. *Seek wisdom from my advisors.*
   b. *Determine if I really want to seek another CEO position.*
   c. *Complete the profile of what I seek in my next position.*
   d. *Determine the kind of training I need and complete it.*
   e. *Create a plan to gain practical experience.*
   f. *Develop my formal search process.*
   g. *Prepare for the interview process.*
   h. *Launch the marketing phase of the plan.*

6. Upon sharing my plan with my key advisors to ask them their advice to refine or enhance my plan and to begin the process, here is my second draft of my Career Strategic Plan.

7. Here is my suggested formal search process:
   a. *Develop talking points for inquiries.*
   b. *Test my introduction letters and resumes.*
   c. *Contact search firms to alert them about my search.*

8. Here is my suggested interview process:
   a. *Research prospective organizations online and by other means.*
   b. *Ask for as much information as possible from targeted organizations.*
   c. *Follow up with key people in the search process.*

Remember to:
   a. Check off your completed work.
   b. Add new components that you discover are needed.
   c. Do a complete review of the plan at least twice a year.

Ralph was wise to look into training opportunities that would help him prepare for a new position. Almost certainly, his new position would entail overseeing a larger organization than he is currently leading. Such an organization would require different operational and management skills, such as more delegating, reporting, and networking.

Ralph knew that developing a formal search process was essential for success. This includes preparing materials such as resumes, cover letters, and follow-up letters. Ralph knew that if he took the time to prepare these materials in advance, they would be much more effective than trying to compile a letter when someone asked for it. Ralph was astute enough to realize, at the same time, that he would have to adapt each of these materials to fit each situation.

He also began to gather some talking points for inquiries by telephone or in person. He was aware that he might forget to mention many of his accomplishments when speaking with someone who was inquiring about his availability. These notes would be pivotal to his success. He liked to communicate by telling stories through the eyes of someone else. He felt that these methods helped him sell himself better and make the accounts more memorable.

Ralph knew that each opportunity to meet with a search committee or an interviewer was important. His objective in each case was to "wow" them with his preparation and how he conducted himself. To accomplish this goal, Ralph knew that he would need to know everything he could about the association and then to find ways to relate his background to its primary needs.

The key element of his campaign would be the marketing phase. Ralph had reached a level that was no longer served by ads in the classifieds. Responding to an occasional ad and alerting search firms to his availability would be part of his plan, but the primary part of this effort would be to search for his future position though networking. Through networking, he would focus on organizations that he had an interest in, he would become much more visible in the right places, and he would keep eyes and ears open for any hint of opportunity.

Ralph Moore's Success Story

Ralph ultimately made the decision to seek a new position. His timeline was not quite correct, but it was pretty close. He developed a profile of what he sought in his next position. His primary goal was to become the CEO of a national organization.

He discovered that most national associations are headquartered in Washington, D.C., and, to a lesser degree, Chicago and New York. As he continued his research, he found that these organizations were much more specialized than he initially thought. They were professional societies for individuals who worked for youth-related organizations or advocacy groups for a particular youth cause.

Ralph found the training he sought through both online and traditional courses. He also found opportunities to talk to CEOs from larger organizations about how they administer their shops. He even asked two CEOs if he could visit their offices to see their operations in person. Ralph felt that both visits were very beneficial, and he even persuaded one of the CEOs to become an advisor.

Ralph created a solid mix of materials including three versions of his resume, one in the form of a curriculum vitae. He prepared for the interview process by conducting extensive research of the organizations that were seeking him. In many cases, he tested his materials with his advisors to make sure that they were effective. Twice his advisors were able to increase the effectiveness of his materials and his approach significantly.

His extensive networking began to pay off. Over a six-month period, four possible positions were discovered, all of them through his network. The opportunities included a trade association that worked with youth organizations, a professional society for youth professionals, a very large regional youth organization, and a national organization whose mission was to encourage youth to be students of history.

Ralph did his homework in researching each association. He discovered that one went through a CEO every three years on average—Ralph immediately dropped that one from his list. Another association had major financial problems. Ralph interviewed with it anyway but ultimately determined that it had too many problems.

The third association was the group whose mission was to encourage history education for youths. Ralph's personal love of history and the fact he had a doctorate in this area made him very curious about this opportunity. Ralph met with the search committee, liked what he saw, and was offered the position.

The fourth association was the large regional youth organization. It was not exactly what Ralph was looking for, but one of his advisors recommended that it might be a good fit nonetheless. Ralph discovered that the organization was huge, with an annual budget of $45 million and an endowment of $75 million. The staff numbered nearly 150 individuals, and the organization was well respected for both its regional and national work. In fact, the organization was cited as a good example for other organizations to follow across the nation. When Ralph interviewed for the position, he felt at home with the search committee. Its members encouraged him to visit the operations office and all of their regional facilities. It was obvious that the leaders of this organization wanted Ralph to become their next CEO, and they offered him a wonderful compensation package.

Ralph took a week to think about these two opportunities. While the history-related association offered a rare opportunity to use his academic and youth-related experience, the regional youth organization offered a position that would make a significant difference. Even though Ralph had set a national organization as his goal, he chose to go with the regional youth organization.

It has been ten years since Ralph decided to become the CEO of the regional youth organization. A lot has happened since then. Since the organization had the financial resources to continue to grow, Ralph gradually became a CEO of the national association. His organization became one of the fasting-growing associations of its kind with facilities and a presence in 47 states. Ralph has become a key player in his field. He is sought after to speak at conferences each year and has written two books that are used throughout his field.

Ralph is now 61 years old. Although he has had a successful career, every once in a while he sits down to update his Career Strategic Plan. Sometimes he thinks he might want to search for another CEO position. Then he just grins and puts his plan back in the file cabinet.

SUMMARY

Section 4: The Career Strategic Plan provides a suggested process to help individuals attain the chief executive officer position of a not-for-profit organization. The materials for this section were based on the findings of the National Study of Not-for-Profit CEOs and the content of the companion book, *The Not-for-Profit CEO: How to Attain & Retain the Corner Office.*

In the study, over 100 CEOs provided their wisdom and personal experience on how they made it to the corner office. Almost all of them noted that they made it to the top by taking charge of their own careers. Yes, they had a lot of help along the way from their advisors and from their network. Many were in the right place at the right time, and they were lucky. Yet being at the right place at the right time is an art.

CEOs or, for that matter, all astute professionals know that you need to be in the game to score. Successful people make it a point to discover where the right place is and to be there at the appropriate time. We can say that successful CEOs are very lucky, but if that is true, it is because they make their own luck. Luck is the discipline of being prepared to act quickly when an opportunity comes your way.

The Career Strategic Plan process is designed to help users enter the game and seize every opportunity that comes up. It encourages busy people to engineer their personal career development concurrently with their ongoing work. The Career Strategic Plan is really the end product of extensive research, self-assessment, and planning. Such a process needs to be part of every individual's game plan, particularly if you aspire to the corner office. You can never start too early; but it is never too late to start, either. Our five examples provide evidence of that:

1. Theresa Rodriguez used the plan to test career areas and to select a course of study in college in not-for-profit administration.
2. Lewis Johnston used the plan to refine his course of study, to extend his outside activities, and to secure his first professional position in a not-for-profit.
3. Frank Fulton used the plan to develop his first successful search for a CEO position.
4. Janet McGuire used the plan to make a successful transition from the for-profit sector to becoming a CEO of a not-for-profit organization.

5. Ralph Moore used the plan to seek greater leadership opportunities as a CEO of a larger association.

Planning your career is important. You should start as early as high school, but you can adapt the planning process at any time in your career. Once you start, career planning should become an intricate part of your professional life.

For most examples, the key to success had nothing to do with complicated theories. The process was simple and straightforward:

- Work harder than everyone else.
- Find ways to be visible.
- Gather together a network of advisors.
- Take control of your career.

The road to the corner office need not be a rocky one. If you are one of the few who wish to position yourself to make a difference in life by becoming a CEO of a not-for-profit organization, a well-designed and a well-executed Career Strategic Plan is a must. It is your career, and it is really up to you to make success possible.

The Volunteer Leadership Role

Techniques don't produce quality products or pick up the garbage on time, people do, people who care, people who are treated as creatively contributing adults.

—Tom Peters

In the companion book to this workbook, *The Not-for-Profit CEO: How to Attain & Retain the Corner Office,* I ended the book with an epilogue titled "A Message to Volunteer Leaders." Its purpose was to emphasize the importance of the relationship that key volunteers play with a not-for-profit CEO and, more importantly, to bring attention to the major responsibility that these individuals have in fully supporting the professional leader.

Throughout this workbook, I emphasized the importance of aspiring CEOs working with volunteers to achieve success. This is an important role for any professional in a not-for-profit organization, and it is one of the primary roles of the CEO. This can be achieved, however, only through a team effort: all of the parties in the relationship working together to achieve a common goal.

As a professional, I have been blessed to work for a number of not-for-profits. I have worked with quality organizations, such as my current association, where the volunteers understand the delicate but important relationship that is needed between them and the CEO and staff. Yet I have also been involved with organizations that never seem to achieve harmony: organizations with dysfunctional professionals and volunteers who did not care, organizations where the volunteers were finding ways to oust the professional leaders, where the professionals or volunteers were out to harm the association itself, and so on. I have never understood such behavior.

Everyone in the process, including professionals and volunteers, needs to put aside personal differences, politics, and agendas and focus on working for the common good. If they do, they can achieve great things. If for some reason they cannot, then they should find other ways to make a contribution to society.

Additional Sources of Information

Source	Find Out About
American Humanics, Inc. 4601 Madison Avenue Kansas City, MO 64112 800-531-6466 *www.humanics.org*	Supports over 70 colleges and universities that offer majors in not-for-profit administration
Union Institute & University 440 East McMillan Street Cincinnati, Ohio 45206-1925 800-486-3116 *www.tui.edu*	Undergraduate and graduate degree programs including a doctoral degree in association management through a partnership with the American Society of Association Executives
American Society of Association Executives 1575 I Street, NW Washington, DC 20005-1103 202-626-2723 *www.asaenet.org*	A host of education programs in association management and the Certified Association Executive (CAE) designation
Association of Fund Raising Professionals 1101 King Street, Suite 700 Alexandria, Virginia 22314 703-684-0410 *www.afpnet.org*	The resource for fundraising information and training
Points of Light Foundation 1400 I Street, Suite 800 Washington, DC 20005 202-729-8000 *www.pointsoflight.org*	The best source for information concerning community service and volunteer issues

About the CD-ROM

INTRODUCTION

This appendix provides you with information on the contents of the CD that accompanies this book. For the latest and greatest information, please refer to the ReadMe file located at the root of the CD.

In This Appendix:

- System Requirements
- Using the CD with Windows
- What You'll Find on the CD
- Troubleshooting

SYSTEM REQUIREMENTS

- A computer with a processor running at 120 Mhz or faster
- At least 32 MB of total RAM installed on your computer; for best performance, we recommend at least 64 MB
- A CD-ROM drive

NOTE: Many popular word processing programs are capable of reading Microsoft Word files. However, users should be aware that a slight amount of formatting might be lost when using a program other than Microsoft Word.

USING THE CD WITH WINDOWS

To install the items from the CD to your hard drive, follow these steps.

1. **Insert the CD into your computer's CD-ROM drive. The license agreement appears.**

The interface won't launch if you have autorun disabled. In that case, click Start@@@>Run. In the dialog box that appears, type D:\start.exe. (Replace D with the proper letter if your CD-ROM drive uses a different letter. If you don't know the letter, see how your CD-ROM drive is listed under My Computer.) Click OK.

2. **Read through the license agreement, and then click the Accept button if you want to use the CD. After you click Accept, the License Agreement window won't appear again.**

The CD interface appears. The interface allows you to install the programs and run the demos with just a click of a button (or two).

WHAT YOU'LL FIND ON THE CD

The following sections are arranged by category and provide a summary of the software and other goodies you'll find on the CD. If you need help with installing the items provided on the CD, refer back to the installation instructions in the preceding section.

Technical Stuff

Shareware programs are fully functional, free, trial versions of copyrighted programs. If you like particular programs, register with their authors for a nominal fee and receive licenses, enhanced versions, and technical support.

Freeware programs are free, copyrighted games, applications, and utilities. You can copy them to as many PCs as you like—for free—but they offer no technical support.

GNU software is governed by its own license, which is included inside the folder of the GNU software. There are no restrictions on distribution of GNU software. See the GNU license at the root of the CD for more details.

Trial, demo, or evaluation versions of software are usually limited either by time or functionality (such as not letting you save a project after you create it).

Content

26 PDF files of all exhibits found in book.

13 blank and customizable forms in Word format—to be filled in by readers.

Any material from the book, including forms, slides, and lesson plans if available, are in the folder named "Content".

Applications

The following applications are on the CD:

- **Adobe Reader.** Adobe Reader is a freeware application for viewing files in the Adobe Portable Document format.

- **Word Viewer.** Microsoft Word Viewer is a freeware viewer that allows you to view, but not edit, most Microsoft Word files. Certain features of Microsoft Word documents may not display as expected from within Word Viewer.

TROUBLESHOOTING

I tried my best to compile programs that work on most computers with the minimum system requirements. Alas, your computer may differ, and some programs may not work properly for some reason.

The two likeliest problems are that you don't have enough memory (RAM) for the programs you want to use, or you have other programs running that are affecting installation or running of a program. If you get an error message such as "Not enough memory" or "Setup cannot continue," try one or more of the following suggestions and then try using the software again:

- **Turn off any antivirus software running on your computer.** Installation programs sometimes mimic virus activity and may make your computer incorrectly believe that it's being infected by a virus.

- **Close all running programs.** The more programs you have running, the less memory is available to other programs. Installation programs typically update files and programs; so if you keep other programs running, installation may not work properly.

- **Have your local computer store add more RAM to your computer.** This is, admittedly, a drastic and somewhat expensive step. However adding more memory can really help the speed of your computer and allow more programs to run at the same time. This may include closing the CD interface and running a product's installation program from Windows Explorer.

Customer Care

If you have trouble with the CD-ROM, please call the Wiley Product Technical Support phone number at (800) 762-2974. Outside the United States, call 1 (317) 572-3994. You can also contact Wiley Product Technical Support at **http://support.wiley.com.** John Wiley & Sons will provide technical support only for installation and other general quality control items. For technical support on the applications themselves, consult the program's vendor or author.

To place additional orders or to request information about other Wiley products, please call (877) 762-2974.

Index

CUSTOMER NOTE: IF THIS BOOK IS ACCOMPANIED BY SOFTWARE, PLEASE READ THE FOLLOWING BEFORE OPENING THE PACKAGE.

This software contains files to help you utilize the models described in the accompanying book. By opening the package, you are agreeing to be bound by the following agreement:

This software product is protected by copyright and all rights are reserved by the author, John Wiley & Sons, Inc., or their licensors. You are licensed to use this software on a single computer. Copying the software to another medium or format for use on a single computer does not violate the U.S. Copyright Law. Copying the software for any other purpose is a violation of the U.S. Copyright Law.

This software product is sold as is without warranty of any kind, either express or implied, including but not limited to the implied warranty of merchantability and fitness for a particular purpose. Neither Wiley nor its dealers or distributors assumes any liability for any alleged or actual damages arising from the use of or the inability to use this software. (Some states do not allow the exclusion of implied warranties, so the exclusion may not apply to you.)